Shadow of the Dragon

Shadow of the Dragon

*Vietnam's Continuing Struggle
with China and Its Implications
for U.S. Foreign Policy*

HENRY J. KENNY

BRASSEY'S
WASHINGTON, D.C.

Text design and composition by World Composition Services, Inc., Sterling, VA.

Cover art derived from: Chinese, Sheath with Bird and Feline or Dragon, Western Han dynasty, 2nd/1st century B.C., jade (nephrite), 10.6 × 5.7 × 0.5 cm, Through prior gifts of Mrs. Chauncey B. Borland, Lucy Maud Buckingham Collection, Emily Crane Chadbourne, Mary Hooker Dole, Edith B. Farnsworth, Mrs. Mary A.B. MacKenzie, Mr. and Mrs. Chauncey B. McCormick, Fowler McCormick, Mrs. Gordon Palmer, Grace Brown Palmer, Chester D. Tripp, et al. Russell Tyson, H.R. Warner, Joseph Winterbotham, and Mr. and Mrs. Edward Ziff, 1987.141front © *The Art Institute of Chicago. All Rights Reserved.*

Library of Congress Cataloging-in-Publication Data
Kenny, Henry.
Shadow of the dragon : Vietnam's continuing struggle with China and the implications for U.S. foreign policy / Henry Kenny.
p. cm.
Includes bibliographical references and index.
ISBN 1-57488-478-6 (hardcover : alk. paper)
ISBN 1-57488-479-4 (pbk : alk. paper)
1. Vietnam—Politics and government. 2. China—Politics and government. 3. United States—Foreign relations—2001–   I. Title.
DS556.58 .K46 2002
327.597051—dc21
2002002650

Printed in the United States of America on acid-free paper that meets the American National Standards Institute Z39-48 Standard.

Brassey's
22841 Quicksilver Drive
Dulles, Virginia 20166

First Edition

10 9 8 7 6 5 4 3 2 1

*This book is dedicated to
all Americans and Vietnamese
who gave their lives for the freedom
and independence of Vietnam.*

TABLE OF CONTENTS

LIST OF MAPS

PREFACE

It has been 34 long years since I left Vietnam on a stretcher aboard a C-141 cargo plane filled with other wounded soldiers. We were stacked three deep in long rows on either side of the aircraft. Many of the men groaned in pain as the plane rumbled down the runway and across the Pacific. Most of us had intravenous lines hooked to blood or medication. Headed for Walter Reed Army Hospital in Washington, D.C., we wondered what awaited us. Some would never walk again, and some would never see again. We had heard that much of the antiwar sentiment in the United States was directed against the military, but to a man we were determined to rebuild our lives as best we could. By the time we reached Andrews Air Force Base outside of Washington, D.C., we were exhausted. The rear ramp of the aircraft lowered to the ground and flight attendants lifted us one by one to the tarmac. As they placed me on the ground, I reached out and tapped the concrete pavement, saying, "God bless America, we're home."

Despite our wounds, we were, in many ways, the lucky ones. Many of our best friends remained in Vietnam, some of them never to return in this life. By the war's end, over 59,000 American men and women had perished in the conflict. They had sacrificed their lives, their youth, and their hopes for love and family on a distant mountain, jungle, or rice paddy. The Vietnam Memorial in Washington, D.C., speaks eloquently for their courage and unheard voices.

Yet the land of Vietnam in which they fought remained, as it had throughout most of the war, something of a mystery. U.S. government leaders had underestimated the tenacity of the foe, the determination of Hanoi, and the difficulty of fighting a people's war on the mainland of Asia. They listed containment of Chinese expansion as one of the principal reasons for entering the war, and paid little attention to the internal dynamics of Vietnamese political, cultural, or social life. They learned the hard way that a long war of attrition required strong domestic support, and when that support eroded, there could be no expectation of victory in combat. Thus it was that Washington, frustrated by the cost and hopelessness of its cause, withdrew its support from South Vietnam just a few years before the great nemesis China, in whose name the war partially was fought, attacked its former protégé in northern Vietnam.

I watched all this from a hospital bed and later from my position as an assistant professor of international relations at West Point. For me Vietnam was a thing of the past, or so I thought. Having gained fluency in the Vietnamese language, however, I soon found myself en route to Hanoi to begin the long and difficult process of accounting for Americans missing in action. During the following 25 years, I continued to visit Vietnam not only on POW/MIA matters but also as an academic at the Institute for International Relations in Hanoi, a business consultant in Hanoi and Saigon (as most Vietnamese still refer to it; it has formally been renamed Ho Chi Minh City), and a researcher on international issues facing Vietnam, most notably its relations with China. In Hanoi I met at various times with the prime minister, the foreign minister, and other national leaders. In discussing Vietnam's relations with China, I interviewed the vice foreign minister, the former minister of justice, senior diplomats and military officials, Communist Party officials, and members of the government concerned with trade and security. I also had the opportunity to talk with the director for China in the foreign ministry and with numerous academics knowledgeable about China. I confess that I was not able to attain the same degree of access in China and relied instead on interviews with visiting officials of the Chinese government, Communist Party, People's Liberation Army, and their supporting institutions.

In completing this work I met with experts on both China and Southeast Asia and wish to thank, in particular, Professor Carlyle Thayer of the Australian Defence Force Academy; Col. Ed O'Dowd, USA (Ret.), former military attaché in China and Vietnam; and Evelyn Colbert, former deputy assistant secretary of state in the Bureau of East Asia and the Pacific. I also wish to give special thanks to the Smith Richardson Foundation for their assistance in making this publication possible.

The manuscript is, of course, my own, and I accept full responsibility for all errors or omissions. I recognize that there are competing points of view, most notably that China will inevitably be the most important power in Asia and will come to dominate the region to such an extent that the relatively smaller and weaker states of Southeast Asia must sooner or late accommodate to Chinese interests. It is my hope that this text will at least cause a reinterpretation of such a viewpoint, especially among those responsible for bringing Vietnam through the twenty-first century.

Dr. Henry J. Kenny
October 2001

CHAPTER 1

Introduction

During the middle of the last century, the United States fought three wars in Asia, all of which were intended to prevent domination of the region by a hostile or potentially hostile power. Today, one of the nations whose armies the United States fought, China, is widely perceived as a rising power that could eventually gain a dominant political, economic, and military position throughout the region. As a result of this perception, many Asian nations are hastening to accommodate Chinese power, even to the extent of sacrificing their traditional national interests. Because of its historic struggle with China for independence, Vietnam is the most conspicuous of these nations.

Having achieved its independence at an enormous and unnecessary price, Hanoi is today at risk of placing that independence in jeopardy by tending to follow the Chinese line, not only in foreign and defense policy, but also in its internal economic and political development. Although there are contrary voices in Vietnam, the tributary relationship that characterized a thousand years of Vietnamese relations with China is once again emerging as a realistic possibility, threatening to absorb the "Smaller Dragon" in a web of control that would be the ultimate betrayal of nationalist ideals for which generations of Vietnamese have fought.

My thesis is that a Vietnamese tributary relationship with China need not reoccur. On the contrary, this book highlights the prospect that the heartbeat of Vietnamese patriotism can lead to another path, one that identifies with both traditional Vietnamese independence and modern global interdependence. There is today in Vietnam a conflict over which path to follow. The United States can influence the outcome

1

of that conflict, but to do so, it must first understand the dynamics of Sino-Vietnamese relations.

The pages that follow attempt to do just that. They explore over 2,000 years of Sino-Vietnamese relations, identify causes and possible consequences of disputes in the South China Sea, evaluate the costs and benefits of current economic relations, examine the direction of political relations, and assess the effect of all of these on U.S. policy.

U.S. policy calls for the promotion of democracy abroad, and to a limited degree this was a motivating factor in U.S. involvement in the Vietnam War. Today, however, the leadership of both China and Vietnam abhor the idea of political pluralism. As in ancient times, when Confucian learning was the hallmark of the Vietnamese political elite, Vietnamese leaders today look to China, with its strong central political control and partial economic reform, as a model for Vietnam's development under the leadership of the Communist Party.

The challenge to U.S. policy under such circumstances is to engage each nation in a way that supports U.S. strategic interests, while simultaneously pushing for human rights and a degree of political pluralism. Perhaps the challenge is too great, as U.S. policy toward Vietnam has tended toward benign neglect, while its policy toward China has oscillated between treating Beijing alternately as a "strategic partner" and as a twenty-first-century cold war antagonist. Neither policy makes much sense. Although the outline of a U.S. policy designed to treat Vietnam as a country and not as a wartime enemy and to integrate China more fully into the international community is in place, the translation of that outline into a pragmatic policy direction requires more attention. This book treats one aspect of such a policy—the influence on the future directions of China and Vietnam that could result from greater understanding of the dynamics of Sino-Vietnamese relations.

The book contains six chapters that address those dynamics. Chapter 2 begins by providing an overview of the importance of the relationship between China and Vietnam for the United States over the past two generations. It points out that while China always loomed large in U.S. policy, Americans tended to see Vietnam as important only in relation to other interests, such as containing Communism or China. It points out that the relationship between China and Vietnam was often misunderstood, and that the series of decisions leading to U.S.

involvement in the Vietnam War were strongly linked to perceived collaboration between the two. Finally, it highlights recent U.S. efforts to appeal to Vietnam's traditional sense of independence and entrepreneurship by providing alternatives to the socialist model that China has become for modern Vietnam.

Chapter 3 addresses the history of Vietnam's relationship with China. It describes Vietnam's extensive interaction with its large neighbor over two millennia, the first under Chinese rule and the second as an independent state. It begins with the mythical origins of Vietnam nearly 5,000 years ago—when the ancestors of modern Vietnamese existed as peoples of the coast and the mountains, far from the reaches of Chinese national power. Later, as the authority of the Middle Kingdom reached southward, these peoples became enmeshed into the fabric of China, absorbing much of its culture and civilization, but also ultimately losing their independent status. They retained, however, their distinctive national traits of hard work, village solidarity, and mistrust of external rule. When the Vietnamese mandarins kowtowed to Chinese sovereigns and exploited the people to their own and Chinese benefit, the people frequently revolted, led by the many heroes of Vietnamese history. China crushed most of these revolts, but eventually the Vietnamese succeeded. After defeating a large Chinese fleet at the Bach Dang River in A.D. 938, Vietnam once again became an independent state.

The chapter describes many Chinese attempts to resubjugate independent Vietnam. For nearly a thousand years, Vietnamese rulers had to pay tribute to the powerful dynasties of China. Often, however, Vietnamese rulers grew corrupt, spawning revolt. On those occasions, the Chinese typically intervened in an attempt to save corrupt and discredited kings loyal to the Chinese emperor. The Vietnamese struggled to defend their precious independence and, in the process, more often than not, defeated the invading Chinese armies. One of the forces enabling Vietnam to succeed in this endeavor was its own southward movement, gradually extending the borders of the country first into the Champa kingdom to its south, and ultimately into Khmer areas of the Mekong Delta, far from the traditional reaches of controlling Chinese influence. But the movement southward also led to cultural and political differences within Vietnam itself, splitting the country between north and south, and providing China additional opportunities to intervene in Vietnamese politics. Those opportunities multiplied when the Western powers intruded onto the scene, but because of the weakness of the later Qing dynasty, China was unable to take advantage of them.

After discussing the French interlude in Vietnam, the chapter analyzes Sino-Vietnamese relations throughout history, concluding that a pattern developed in their relationship that repeated itself with minor variations for over 2,000 years. It describes that pattern in terms of an asymmetric relationship between the two states, leading to a vicious cycle, which alternated between Vietnamese accommodation and tribute on the one hand and revolt and military victory on the other. It concludes by suggesting a way for Vietnam to break that cycle and become truly independent in its domestic and international policies.

Chapter 4 examines land border and South China Sea disputes between China and Vietnam. It first reviews events leading to the land border agreement of late 1999, and also the issues and process leading to the agreement to demarcate the Gulf of Tonkin at the end of 2000. It then focuses on the Paracel Islands, which both countries claim in their entirety, and relates these claims to those of both countries in the Spratly Islands, parts of which the Philippines, Malaysia, and Taiwan also claim. Finally, it discusses Sino-Vietnamese competition in adjacent petroleum exploration blocks in the Con Son Basin, off the continental shelf of southern Vietnam. In all four areas there is an effort to explain the nature of the disputes, analyzing what is at stake in terms of sovereignty, ocean resources, sea-lanes, and international prestige.

Following examination of Sino-Vietnamese disputes in the South China Sea are two chapters focusing on the economic and political benefits that Vietnamese leaders currently perceive in their warmer relationship with China. While the leadership in Hanoi and the people of Vietnam do not equally share these perceptions, they shape the nature of an evolving relationship in which the goals of economic development and political stability are paramount.

In keeping with these goals, chapter 5 describes how delegation after delegation travels from Vietnam to Beijing to express profound admiration and praise for the Chinese economic system, which they extol as a model for future Vietnamese development. The delegations also encourage increased bilateral trade and Chinese investment in Vietnam, while thanking their hosts for Chinese economic assistance. The chapter questions the motivation of the Vietnamese leadership in establishing this "student to teacher" type relationship, especially in view of the fact that Chinese economic assistance pales in comparison to that of other international donors. It also questions the advisability of modeling the Vietnamese economic system on that of China.

Chapter 6 examines the same issues from a political point of view. It points out that the relative disparity in size will always mean that an asymmetric relationship will exist between these two nations. While the exact nature of that asymmetric relationship remains unclear, the geographic proximity of Vietnam to China, its relative economic and military inferiority,[1] and the shadow of history impel Vietnam to some form of accommodation with China. It points to a Chinese ambition to control the foreign and defense policies of its most immediate neighbor to the south, and therein signals the rest of Asia that China is the rising power to which they all must sooner or later accommodate. The chapter points out that neither Vietnam nor China serves to gain from renewed conflict, but that the fact of relatively greater Chinese economic and military strength does not compel Vietnam to accommodate to the point of establishing a renewed tributary relationship with the Middle Kingdom. While recognizing that China will always be important in Vietnamese policy, the chapter offers alternatives for Vietnam, both externally in its foreign policy, and internally in its path of economic and political development. It concludes that in this era of globalization, economic and political forces emanating from more distant lands are just as important to the future of Vietnam as those of nearby China.

The seventh chapter examines the implications of future Sino-Vietnamese relations on U.S. interests and policy in Asia. Chinese actions and statements indicate three concerns with U.S.-Vietnam relations. First, the development of close U.S.-Vietnamese relations could help undermine the Chinese policy of gaining increased influence in Southeast Asia. Second, any U.S. military-to-military relationship with Vietnam could legitimize the U.S. forward presence in Asia. Third and finally, U.S. influence on Vietnam could result in economic and political reforms that could ultimately challenge the priorities, if not the legitimacy, of the Communist Party.

Taking these Chinese concerns into account, the chapter explores four plausible scenarios in Sino-Vietnamese relations—those characterized by conflict, alliance, tribute, and a due respect for China. It analyzes the factors favoring each of these different scenarios, including national culture, national independence, relative national power, stability in the South China Sea, political ideology, regime maintenance, and economic benefit. It then analyzes each scenario in terms of U.S. objectives—which scenario best favors American interests in peace and stability, free trade and investment, respect for human rights, and political pluralism. Based on this analysis, it provides conclusions and recommendations for U.S. policy.

Finally, chapter 8 presents the overall conclusions derived from earlier chapters. It discusses a vision for the future of Sino-Vietnamese relations and the role the United States may play in facilitating a freer and more truly independent Vietnam.

CHAPTER 2

China, Vietnam, and U.S. Policy in Perspective

A generation has passed since the caskets came home from Vietnam. Just a few years before, most of the young men in those caskets had never heard of the land in which they died. Before the war Vietnam was as remote from the minds of the American public as it has once again become in the twenty-first century. But as the war unfolded, gradually at first and then with increasing ferocity, "Vietnam" became not only a household word but also a place that haunted the American psyche, as it continues to do with countless veterans who fought there. During the Tet Offensive of 1969, over 500 young Americans lost their lives in combat each week. At the battle of Hamburger Hill a year later, 70 Americans paid the ultimate price. At Khe Sanh, there were another 600.[1] The Vietnam War wall in Washington, D.C., listing the names of the missing and the dead, attests to the sacrifice these young soldiers made over a 17-year period. During those years, whatever one's opinion of the war, Vietnam was perceived as of the utmost importance to the United States, if only because we were there.[2]

The Vietnam of today, however, is relatively insignificant to U.S. policymakers. For most Americans, the Vietnam of today is of no concern, and the Vietnam of yesterday is viewed primarily as a battleground, a foreign policy or military blunder that cost the United States heavily. China, in contrast, has assumed an almost dominating role in U.S. policy toward East Asia. While China has always been of great importance to the United States, the end of the cold war and the perceived rise of Chinese political, economic, and military power have focused U.S. attention on Chinese policy and strategy. A host of unresolved issues cry out for attention: how to prevent China from taking rash action against Taiwan, how to more fully integrate China into the world community of nations, how to avoid a twenty-first-century arms race with China, how to persuade China to abide by the Missile Technology Control Regime, how to promote human rights in China, how to protect U.S. nuclear and military technology from China, and how to protect U.S. intellectual property rights in China, among others.

Yet, despite the current overarching importance of China relative to Vietnam for U.S. interests, both countries, in the recent past, have been at the heart of U.S. policy concerns in Asia and may become so again. In one sense, Vietnam was responsible for U.S. entry into World War II. When the Japanese Imperial Army entered Vietnam in 1941, President Franklin D. Roosevelt imposed an oil embargo on Japan, leading directly to Tokyo's decision to attack Pearl Harbor. Like the U.S. involvement in the Vietnam War a generation later, the U.S. action had little to do with Vietnam itself, but with its relationship to surrounding areas—in this case British Malaya, for which Vietnam was seen as a stepping-stone. In 1941 Britain was a truly vital partner for the United States in Europe, and a Japanese takeover of Malaya, with its rubber plantations and tin mines, was seen as unacceptable to Britain's war effort.

Likewise, China played a key role in the policy and strategy of the United States during World War II. A haven for U.S. bombers during the famous James Doolittle raid on Tokyo in 1942, China also became a second front against the Japanese Imperial Army. However, in a harbinger of America's failure to understand Asia a generation later in Vietnam, the United States provided military support for Chiang Kai-shek's Nationalists in China without demanding accountability and responsibility for how that support was used. In his insightful book explaining the limits of U.S. aid to China, General "Vinegar" Joe Stilwell, who was responsible for implementing that aid, described how much of it was wasted as he tried to leverage it to reform Chiang's administration.[3]

After the war, China became the center of heated policy debate in Washington over whether and how to assist the Nationalists against the People's Liberation Army (PLA) under Mao Zedong. After Chiang's evacuation to Taiwan, the debate shifted for several years to "who lost

China," and subsequently to the degree of political and military support the United States should offer to Taiwan. As recently as 1996, in response to China's firing of missiles in waters surrounding Taiwan, the United States sent two carrier battle groups to within air-striking range of the island. Although the vicissitudes of international relations in Asia may lead to a settlement of the issue, tension between China and Taiwan is likely to remain at the top of U.S. policy concern in Asia for decades to come.

China was also the focus of U.S. attention during the Korean War. The debates over whether the PLA would enter the war if United Nations forces entered North Korea, whether to bomb China in retaliation if they did, and under what conditions to terminate conflict with the PLA, all absorbed U.S. policymakers. Between 1950 and 1953, the United States lost over 37,000 men in Korea. Most of those casualties resulted from direct combat with the PLA, which itself lost over 500,000 men at the hands of the UN forces.

Then, of course, there was the Chinese role in the war in Vietnam. Like the U.S. involvement in Korea, the U.S. commitment in Vietnam was seen in large part as an effort to contain the perceived expansion of China and Communist ideology in Asia. Over 59,000 Americans died in the war, many at the hands of Chinese-made small arms or mines. Over 100,000 Chinese military advisers aided North Vietnam during the war, and the possibility of China's entering the war, as it had in Korea, kept the United States from sending ground forces into North Vietnam. In this sense, China sealed the U.S. defeat in Vietnam, because the war became, as former South Vietnamese premier Nguyen Cao Ky once stated, like a football game in which the U.S. team could not cross the 50-yard line.[4]

With U.S recognition of the People's Republic of China in 1979, U.S. interests in China shifted to a cold war framework in which China was seen as a means to pressure the Soviet Union into a less-threatening posture. The 1980s saw development of political, economic, and military ties with China designed in part to limit the power and influence of Moscow. At the same time, U.S. nonrecognition of Vietnam helped isolate that country and added to Chinese pressure on Hanoi to withdraw its military forces from Cambodia. American business ties with China also accelerated, and bilateral trade grew an average 19 percent annually between 1985 and 2000.[5]

During the same period, Vietnam receded into the background of U.S. policy concerns. As Vietnam was before the war there, it appeared to be a zone of neither potential crisis nor great economic benefit to the United States. It thus became far removed from the minds of U.S. policymakers. They supported the Association of Southeast Asian Nations (ASEAN) and China in condemning Vietnam for its occupation of Cambodia. They cheered after their new friend, China, sent troops across the border to "teach Vietnam a lesson" in 1979. They criticized Vietnam for its insufficient cooperation on POW/MIA issues, and they supported keeping Vietnam from membership in international financial institutions. Finally in 1995, after Vietnam's withdrawal from Cambodia, improvements on POW/MIA accountability, and limited economic and social reforms, the United States established diplomatic relations with Vietnam—16 years after doing so with China.

Nevertheless, Vietnam may once again become important in U.S. policy, not only because of its future in Southeast Asia, but also because it may, over time, be able to influence the future direction of China. Beginning in the latter half of the 1990s, Americans saw that direction in increasingly negative terms, as an assertive China not only pressured Taiwan, but also sought a sphere of influence in Asia, including Vietnam, at the expense of the "hegemon," as Beijing now labels the United States. In December 2000 General Hugh Shelton, then chairman of the Joint Chiefs of Staff, identified potential Chinese hostility as a major concern, and in that context indicated that the United States military must remain strong. At the same time, citing U.S. intelligence gaps with respect to China, the Pentagon reported to the Congress that defending Taiwan was a matter of "grave concern" for the United States.[6]

By the time that the Clinton administration ended, a portrait of a China with growing economic and military power, acting against the interests of the United States, had reemerged. As President George W. Bush took office, it appeared that China could well be the single most important foreign and defense policy challenge not only for his administration, but also for the United States in the twenty-first century.

Understanding all the ways and means of influencing China is thus a critical challenge for U.S. policymakers. As indicated, one of those ways may be through Vietnam. It is generally assumed, because of its size, relative modernization, and social and cultural similarity to Vietnam, that China should serve as the model for its smaller neighbor to the south. Just as China sought to "teach Vietnam a lesson" by its border invasion in 1979, the China of today is teaching Vietnam a lesson in political and economic development by extolling limited economic reforms under the strong leadership of the Communist Party. But the thesis of this book questions this assumption. It raises the possibility that, by choosing a developmental path quite different from that of China, Vietnam may, in succeeding decades, become the teacher rather than the pupil.

The likelihood of this possibility appears remote in today's political environment, but there are three reasons for considering it a realistic possibility. First, Vietnam is free to choose its own developmental path. Its internal politics are not, except by the choice of its own leaders, under the sway and strong influence of Beijing. Second, Vietnam may follow any of the ample alternate models in Asia that, over the years, have outpaced China in socioeconomic performance. Taiwan is one example, but postwar progress in Japan, South Korea, and several of the ASEAN states provide many others. Last, there is Vietnam's relationship with the United States. In some ways, this is something of a love-hate relationship, but there are plenty of times in recent Vietnamese history when Hanoi expressed the most ardent admiration for the United States—its Declaration of Independence, its political stability, its military power, and its dynamic economy.

Despite parroting the Chinese line in condemning the U.S. bombing of the Chinese embassy in Belgrade, "interfering" in internal affairs of other nations by promoting human rights, and demanding "unreasonable" reforms as the price of economic ties, there exists in Vietnam today a reservoir of goodwill toward the United States. With an educated U.S. policy toward Vietnam, the United States at least has the potential to tap that reservoir in guiding Vietnam toward a different and more successful developmental path in the twenty-first century.

Development of U.S. Policy toward Vietnam

If U.S. policy toward Vietnam is one potential way of influencing China, then a review of U.S. policy and its development is thus important to understanding whether and how that potential might be realized. The review that follows begins with post–World War II U.S. policy toward Vietnam and relates it to core U.S. interests over the long term. In so doing, it concludes that the goals of U.S. policy have been remarkably consistent for over two generations.

Although it can be argued that the United States had a policy toward Vietnam when it was still part of French-controlled Indochina, or during the war when a few men from the Office of Strategic Services trained a few Viet Minh guerrillas, the first clearly articulated U.S. policy came in 1944 while the region was under Japanese control. That year President Roosevelt handed his aide a note that stated: "I don't want the French back in Indochina."[7] Unfortunately for Vietnam and, ultimately, the United States, this policy direction died with the president in 1945. French forces reentered Vietnam in 1946 and for eight years fought to retain their former colonial possession.

Whether reflecting the anticolonial or the anti-French proclivities of the late president, the Harry S. Truman administration did not support aid to the French war effort until early 1950. Although the United States might have intervened against Ho Chi Minh, because he was a known Communist, French forces seemed totally adequate to their tasks, and the Viet Minh appeared as a united front organization. More important, the United States was absorbed with domestic development and the reconstruction of Europe and had little or no interest in supporting the French war effort.

In late 1949 and early 1950, three events occurred that changed U.S. policy from one of benign neglect to support of the French. The first was Mao's victory in China and his subsequent support for the Viet Minh, resulting in French defeats on the battlefield, particularly along the China border. The second was a clearer identification of the Viet Minh with international Communism at a time of great concern about that subject. After diplomatic recognition by China and the Soviet Union in January 1950, the Democratic Republic of Vietnam under Ho had immediately announced its support for Communist "liberation" of Cambodia.[8] As a precursor to the domino theory, these actions shaped the attitude of the United States toward the First Indochina War but did not by themselves alter U.S. policy. Washington changed its policy only because of a third factor that had nothing do with events in Indochina itself. At the beginning of 1950, President Truman authorized military assistance for French Indochina, because the French asserted that, unless that assistance was forthcoming, their ability to fulfill Allied military commitments in Europe would be seriously jeopardized.[9]

While the military aid was small at first, France easily persuaded U.S. policymakers that the two countries were fighting the same enemy once the war in Korea began. By 1954 the United States was paying 78 percent of French war costs and U.S. airmen were kicking "door bundles" of military supplies by parachute to besieged French forces at Dien Bien Phu.[10] U.S. aid did not include U.S. military forces, however, as the prevailing attitude of a Joint Chiefs of Staff memorandum reveals: "Indochina is devoid of decisive military objectives and the allocation of more than token U.S. armed forces in Indochina would be a serious diversion of limited U.S. capabilities."[11]

With the division of Vietnam after the Geneva Convention of 1954, U.S. policy shifted to provide limited and conditional military and economic aid to the fledgling government of South Vietnam under Ngo Dinh Diem. The aid began in January 1955, and for three years combined military and economic aid totaled over $300 million annually. The Dwight D. Eisenhower administration, although viewing the aid as needed to fight Communism, was skeptical of its ultimate utility, with Secretary of State John Foster Dulles justifying it "if only to buy time to build strength elsewhere in the region."[12] The president himself wrote to Ngo Dinh Diem that the aid was predicated upon his performance and that it was to be limited in size and duration. Eisenhower meant what he said, and as Diem became more autocratic, the president cut U.S. aid by a hundred million dollars during his last year in office.[13]

In summary, the United States provided aid throughout the pre–Vietnam War period, first to the French and then to the government of the Republic of Vietnam (South Vietnam), as a calculated gamble to check the expansion of Communism in Asia. Implicitly this meant checking the expansion of the Chinese brand of Communism. In this view, Viet Minh and Viet Cong success resulted in large part from Chinese aid, a perception that challenged the commitment of the United States to similarly aid its friends in Indochina.[14] Should Chinese aid prove more effective than that of the United States, the implications for the rest of Southeast Asia were seen as dire—Vietnam was seen as a test case of U.S. versus Chinese ability and determination to affect the political future of the entire region.[15]

During the 1960s, as has been well documented, this view persisted and became much more serious as the Viet Cong gained in strength and President John Kennedy extended the test case thesis to all developing nations. U.S. policy toward Vietnam became absorbed into the cold war as part of the challenge of "wars of national liberation." Before becoming president, Kennedy had gone so far as to declare that "Vietnam represents the cornerstone of the Free World in Southeast Asia, the keystone to the arch, the finger in the dike. Burma, Thailand, India, Japan, the Philippines and, obviously, Laos and Cambodia are among those whose security would be threatened if the red tide of Communism overflowed into Vietnam."[16]

The Lyndon Johnson administration inherited the policy at a time when the armed forces of South Vietnam were failing to meet the challenge. Although Kennedy, a month before his death, gave indications that U.S. support was contingent upon better performance by Saigon, President Johnson lifted the limits and ordered U.S troops "to the rescue."[17] Explaining the U.S. involvement, the president stressed that "America keeps her word . . . we are steadfast in a policy that has been followed for ten years in three administrations."[18] By the end of his administration, Johnson had over 500,000 U.S. troops in Vietnam, justifying them as follows: "Our purpose in Vietnam is to prevent the success of aggression. It is not conquest; it is not empire; it is not foreign bases; it is not domination. It is, simply put, just to prevent the forceful conquest of South Vietnam by North Vietnam."[19]

Although President Johnson tried to do whatever was necessary to attain that goal, the pressure of public opinion forced him, in March 1968, to announce a policy shift to a more limited form of support for South Vietnam. He cut General William Westmoreland's large troop request by more than 90 percent and declared a bombing halt over North Vietnam.[20] Three days later Hanoi announced its willingness to open talks with the United States, leading to the long and arduous Paris peace talks that culminated in 1973.[21] During the interval, President Richard Nixon continued Johnson's limited support for South Vietnam, augmenting his "plan to end the war" by retraining and equipping its army in a process of "Vietnamization." In a throwback to the final Kennedy policy of 1963, he articulated a "Nixon Doctrine," through which the United States would furnish military and economic assistance "but look to the nation directly threatened to assume the primary responsibility of its own defense."[22] In 1975, two years after the Paris accords, South Vietnam proved unable to do so against an invasion from the north.

After Saigon fell, U.S. policymakers did not want to have anything to do with Vietnam. Secretary of State Henry Kissinger told the first congressional delegation to visit Hanoi not to offer Vietnam anything, because, he said, in three years Vietnam would come begging to the United States. In a sense, it did not take three years, as the Vietnamese side in December 1975 presented the delegation its expectations of $3.25 billion from the United States "to heal the wounds of war" as "promised" in a secret letter from President Nixon.[23] The U.S. side refused to even consider the proposal, in part because it was concocted in secret, but mainly because it was contingent on Hanoi's adhering to the Paris Peace Agreement of 1973, which did not happen, and the approval of the Congress, which could not happen in the political environment of the time. In mid-1977 Hanoi finally dropped its "demand" for contributions "to heal the wounds of war," opening a window of opportunity for normalization of relations with the United States that lasted until Vietnam's invasion of Cambodia in late 1978.[24]

U.S. policy adamantly opposed Vietnam's invasion of Cambodia. Hanoi was seen as the aggressor, with ambitions to control all of Indochina. Moreover, the Soviet Union, the main antagonist of the United States in the cold war, had signed a treaty of friendship and cooperation with Hanoi just before Vietnam invaded Cambodia and provided financial and diplomatic support for the occupation over the next 10 years. On at least two occasions during that period, Vietnamese forces crossed the Thai border in hot pursuit of forces of the Khmer Rouge, the regime that the Vietnamese had ousted from power in Cambodia. Until Vietnam's withdrawal from Cambodia in 1988, therefore, its occupation of the country served as a major obstacle to normalization of relations with the United States.

The principal obstacle to normalization, however, remained Vietnam's reluctance to provide all the information and bodily remains it had of Americans missing as a result of the war. Expert witnesses testified that Vietnam had a warehouse in which the remains of some 400 persons believed to be Americans were kept, to be doled out as sweeteners to various U.S. delegations that could influence U.S. policy.[25] To address the issue, President George Bush established a road map for normalization of relations, in which Vietnamese cooperation on Cambodia and POW/MIA matters was the key to U.S. steps toward normalization. Hanoi took these matters seriously, for normalization meant not only a way to help overcome its international political isolation, but it also offered the possibility of trade and investment that could resuscitate its moribund economy. In the late 1980s, therefore, having seriously weakened the Khmer Rouge, Vietnam withdrew from Cambodia and began to improve its efforts to account for missing Americans.[26]

Normalization finally occurred in 1995. POW/MIA matters continued as a high priority in U.S. policy, but nonwar factors also emerged as crucial to the bilateral relationship.[27] Among them were human rights, trade and investment, and Vietnam's relations with its neighbors. "We must look to the future and not to the past" was the hallmark of foreign ministry remarks to visiting Americans. The U.S. embassy in Hanoi opened in 1995, and in 1997 the first U.S. ambassador, former POW and congressman Douglas (Pete) Peterson, took his post. In September 2000 the United States and Vietnam agreed to terms for normal trade relations, and in November 2000 Bill Clinton became the first U.S. president since Richard Nixon to visit Vietnam.[28]

It appeared from these events that U.S. relations with Vietnam were on track and that the track would lead to a better future for both countries. Washington continued to favor democracy in Vietnam but did so primarily by criticizing Vietnam's human rights record and stressing the advantages that U.S. trade and investment might have in bringing Vietnam toward a more pluralistic political system. The U.S. trade representative, for example, pointed to the political advantages of trade as follows:

> Our trade agreements (with Vietnam, Laos, and Cambodia) make a contribution to economic reform and the rule of law in commercial areas in these countries. In doing so they tend over time to reduce arbitrary state power, offer individuals greater economic opportunities and more freedom to determine their own future, complementing, although in no way substituting for, our human rights initiatives.[29]

President Clinton reiterated these thoughts, stating that "we hope expanded trade will go hand in hand with strength and respect for human rights and labor standards. For we live in an age where wealth is generated by the free exchange of ideas and stability depends on democratic choices."[30] During his visit to Vietnam in November 2000, President Clinton likewise expressed the hope that democracy would one day be part of Vietnam's future.

For the immediate future, however, any U.S. hope for democracy in Vietnam rests with the political leadership in Hanoi. Unlike many Vietnamese business and foreign affairs experts, that leadership, today more than ever, looks not to the United States, but to China as a political model. Any U.S. policy that aspires to a more democratic Vietnam runs directly counter to their view of China as a model for the future of Vietnam. It is the purpose of this book, therefore, to examine Vietnam's relationship with China in all its facets, evaluating the dynamics that impel Vietnam toward China, but also those that encourage it to redirect its enormous energies into alternative paths of socioeconomic development. China will always play a large role in Vietnam's calculation of its national interests, but U.S. policy can also play a role, helping offset a current Vietnamese tendency to return to historic patterns of overreliance on China in choosing its direction for the twenty-first century.

Looking to the Future

On 17 November 2000 President Bill Clinton addressed an audience at the Vietnam National University in Hanoi. In that speech the president noted the shared suffering of the two countries in the past and the need to look to the future. "Today, the United States and Vietnam open a new chapter in our relationship, at a time when people all across the world trade more, travel more, know more about and talk more with each other than ever before. Even as people take pride in their national independence, we know we are becoming more and more interdependent."

Continuing with a description of the implications of globalization on Vietnam, the president went on to say that globalization is inevitable and that Vietnam, like other nations, will need to set national policies that optimize its benefits and minimize its risks. While pointing out that the United States cannot and will not impose its ideals on Vietnam, he stressed that the American experience with political, economic, and social freedom has enabled it to formulate just such effective national policies.

> For example, we have seen that economies work better where newspapers are free to expose corruption, and independent courts can ensure that contracts are honored, that competition is robust and fair, that public officials honor the rule of law.
>
> In our experience, guaranteeing the right to religious worship and the right to political dissent does not threaten the stability of a society. . . . In our experience young people are much more likely to have confidence in their future if they have a say in shaping it, in choosing their governmental leaders and having a government that is accountable to those it serves.[31]

The president's speech was noteworthy for a couple reasons. First, it focused on the future. In this regard, it echoed Vietnamese expressions of hope for a better relationship with the United States dating back a generation. "We must look to the future, and not the past, in building a better lives for ourselves and our children," Premier Pham Van Dong had told a visiting congressional delegation as early as 1975.[32] More important, the president's speech approached Vietnam with the hope that its future direction would follow the path of freedom pioneered by the United States. "Only you can decide if you will continue to open your markets, open you [sic] society and strengthen the rule of law. Only you can decide how to weave individual liberties and human rights into the rich and strong fabric of Vietnamese national identity."[33]

The president's speech is also noteworthy because it clearly conflicts with the policies of the leaders of the People's Republic of China. For them it is an example of U.S. intrusion into the internal affairs of a neighboring friendly country. Moreover, the fact that the president of the United States was visiting Vietnam may have been seen as part of a U.S. strategy of enhancing ties with China's Southeast Asian neighbors, clearly challenging Beijing's overall strategy of shaping these countries' foreign and defense policies. Coming on the heels of the March 2000 visit to Vietnam by his secretary of defense, the president's visit also conflicted with Beijing's policy of steadily improving its relations with

Southeast Asian countries as a means of delegitimizing the presence of U.S. military forces in the region.

Adhering to this Chinese line, senior Vietnamese Communist Party leaders were negative toward the visit, announcing it only two days before the president's arrival, canceling a news conference by the foreign minister the day before Clinton's arrival, and castigating the United States for its history of "aggression" in meetings with President Clinton.[34] From the perspective of most Vietnamese, however, the visit represented ties with the United States that they see as beneficial for the future of their country. Government officials saw it as a step toward eliciting U.S. foreign assistance, foreign ministry officials as enhancing their efforts to build a multidirectional foreign policy, reformers as stimulating needed changes in the economic system, and the population as a nebulous hope for political change.

The challenge of an opening to the United States, from the Vietnamese party leadership perspective, is how to exploit the benefits of such ties without eroding its power base. This is not an easy problem for Hanoi to solve, and it is a major reason for Vietnam to follow the Chinese path of modernization, specifically allowing for limited economic liberalization while retaining strong central control by the Communist Party. At the same time, Vietnam is becoming concerned that the benefits of the Chinese path may be exaggerated, while the risks for Vietnam in following that path may be more than it bargained for, particularly if China attempts to reassert its position as the Middle Kingdom of modern Asia.

CHAPTER 3

The Historical Legacy

By far the most important international relationship for Vietnam over the past 2,000 years has been that with China, its colossal neighbor to the north. Vietnam was immensely influenced by China, and for over 1,000 years, from 111 B.C. until A.D. 938, with the exception of some short-lived revolts, it lost its independence to the Middle Kingdom. Still, the Vietnamese people's desire for independence was never eradicated, and time after time Vietnamese patriots led rebellions against their Chinese masters. Finally, in A.D. 938 Vietnam gained its precious independence from China, and with some interruption, it has maintained this independence to this day.

Yet even after Vietnam became independent, Chinese political, cultural, and economic influence persisted to such an extent that the very identity of Vietnam as a nation was frequently cast in terms of its separateness from China. That separateness included some unique cultural characteristics, but its essence is perhaps best understood by words ascribed to Ho Chi Minh: "nothing is more precious than freedom and independence."[1]

China's view of its relationship with Vietnam, conversely, was that its southern neighbor was not that important in either its internal affairs or its grand strategy for the defense and development of the Middle Kingdom. The Vietnamese were "barbarians" like other surrounding non-Chinese peoples, except that they emulated Chinese culture to a greater extent, and insisted on a degree of independence that occasionally infringed on Peking's (Beijing's) prerogatives of sovereignty. The only important point for China was to ensure that Vietnam did nothing to oppose the supremacy of China in the hierarchy of Asian kingdoms. This meant setting limits on Vietnam's zeal for independence and ensuring that it acknowledged Chinese authority and did nothing to challenge China's dominant role in Asia.

This chapter describes the historic relationship between these two countries. It does so by focusing first on the outlines of that history—the important persons and events that shaped that nature of the relationship over the past 2,000 years. It then analyzes the principal themes that occurred and recurred as the two nations struggled in pursuit of their respective destinies. It concludes by suggesting that Sino-Vietnamese relations today are largely shaped by many of those same themes, and that the future of their relationship will be part of the continuum described.

Historical Overview of Sino-Vietnamese Relations

According to Vietnamese legend, Vietnam's prehistory included a kingdom known as Van Lang (2879–258 B.C.). The legend has it that the great-grandson of the Chinese king, Shen Nung (2838–2698 B.C.), married an immortal, whose youngest son, Loc Tuc, ruled a kingdom that included what is now China's Guangxi Autonomous Region and Guangdong Province and northern Vietnam. The lowland area of this kingdom was known as Lac Viet and was ruled by the mythical Loc Long Quan, sometimes claimed by some to be the son of Loc Tuc and by others to be the son of a mountain god and a water goddess. Loc Long Quan married the daughter of a mountain king in southern China, the beautiful princess Au Co, who delivered a pouch of eggs from which came 100 sons.

Needless to say, this situation presented problems to the young couple, and because of Loc Long Quan's affinity for the lowlands and Au Co's penchant for the mountains, they agreed to separate, with each taking 50 sons to these respective regions. Vietnamese schoolbooks today cite the 50 sons with Loc Long Quan as the ancestors of fishermen and those living by the coast and the 50 sons with Au Co as the ancestors of the mountain people. Both the mountaineers and the coastal people, according to this legend, have Chinese ancestors.[2]

China's Southward Movement and the First Vietnamese Historical Kingdom

From the ninth to the fourth centuries B.C., Chinese culture and authority spread southward, and by the third century they reached the Red (Hong) River delta. In 258 B.C., Thuc Phan, reputed to be the king of Tay Au in China's present-day Guangxi Autonomous Region, conquered Van Lang and established the kingdom of Au Lac, with Co Loa, a dozen miles from present-day Hanoi, as his capital. A few years later, during the reign of Shih Huang Ti (246–209 B.C.), the "first emperor" of the Ch'in dynasty, General Chao T'o conquered the then Kwangsi (Guangxi) and Kwangtung (Guangdong) regions and annexed them to China. Their population at the time was non-Chinese, made up of peoples related to the T'ais and the Vietnamese.[3] In 207 B.C. Trieu Da, a Chinese general who broke with the Ch'in emperor, seized the opportunity presented by the weak Chinese dynasty to subjugate Au Lac. He named his new kingdom Nam Viet. Vietnamese today look to Nam Viet, and its antecedent Au Lac, as proof of their historical independence from China. (See map 3-1.)

A year after Trieu Da established Nam Viet, the Ch'in dynasty collapsed. Trieu Da seized the opportunity by proceeding to divorce Nam Viet from Chinese influence. Among his many acts to assert total independence from China, he:[4]

- Proclaimed himself king of the independent state of Nam Viet
- Severed ties with China
- Killed all his subjects loyal to the emperor
- Expanded his area of control in the present-day Chinese regions of Guangxi Autonomous Region and Guangdong Province, as well as in northern Vietnam
- Moved the capital of Nam Viet to Phien Ngu (near what was once known as Canton and that is now known as Guangzhou)
- Required immigrants from China to adopt local Vietnamese customs

The Chinese referred to this new kingdom as Nan Yueh, or "southern barbarians" (south of the Yangtze River).[5] This pejorative term was a harbinger of trouble for a kingdom that had so studiously distanced itself from its northern neighbor.

Map 3.1. Ancient Nam Viet before Its Conquest by China in 111 B.C.

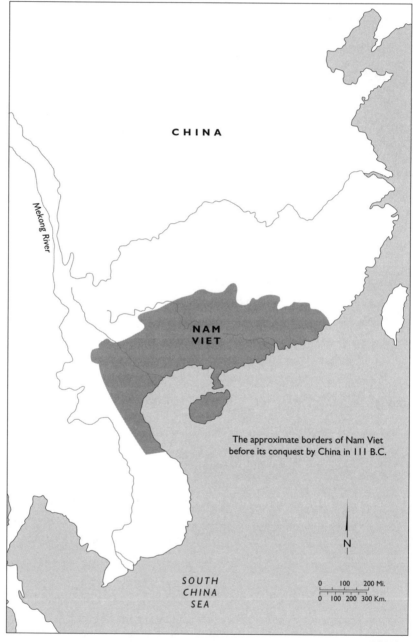

CHINA

Mekong River

NAM VIET

The approximate borders of Nam Viet before its conquest by China in 111 B.C.

N

SOUTH CHINA SEA

0   100   200 Mi.
0   100 200 300 Km.

Bill Nelson

Trouble was not long in coming. In the second century B.C., the new and powerful Han dynasty expanded its authority southward at a rapid rate. In 111 B.C. Emperor Wu Ti, "the creator of Chinese imperialism in Asia," annexed the kingdom of Nam Viet.[6] At the time Nam Viet was a feudal kingdom. Its lords accommodated to the Chinese rule because, in doing so, they were able, at first, to retain their local economic and political power.

Chinese Rule: 111 B.C.–A.D. 938

The thousand years of Chinese rule over Vietnam began with little change in the life of the average Vietnamese. While their lords paid homage to the Chinese governor, life on the farm and in the villages varied but little.

All this changed dramatically at the beginning of the new millennium. Between A.D. 1 and 25, Sinicization of the Vietnamese began in earnest. Men were required to grow long hair and women to wear pants instead of skirts. Chinese immigration accelerated, including numerous learned men who taught the indigenous people more advanced Chinese methods of agriculture and organized the local administration along Chinese lines.[7]

Scholar D. G. E. Hall writes that "The recruitment of a militia of the Chinese type and the creation of a subordinate civil service of indigenous officials threatened the traditional feudal structure of society. . . . Chinese immigration was stepped up, and the policy of assimilation was adopted. Chinese studies were organized, and indigenous scholars sat for the Chinese examinations leading to the mandarinate. Chinese became the official language and the language of the Vietnamese intellectual elite. There was also some miscegenation between the indigenes and the Chinese."[8]

As time went on, Chinese rule became increasingly harsh. Vietnamese peasants were taxed and had to contribute labor to public works projects. Local lords lost power to a more intrusive Chinese administrative system. Some Vietnamese feared that they were losing their sense of national identity, and like American patriots at the Second Continental Congress, aspired to freedom from foreign rule and the presence of foreign soldiers in their midst.[9] A noted scholar of Vietnam expressed the transition thusly: "Thanks to Chao To [Trieu Da], Chinese culture was forsaken and the Chinese immigrants adopted local customs and became more and more Vietnamese. But later, when the Han and the T'ang Sinicized the local people, the Vietnamese aristocracy became more and more Chinese."[10]

It was under these conditions that local Vietnamese leaders revolted. In A.D. 39 Trung Trac, whose husband had been killed by the Chinese, and her sister led a rebellion against Chinese rule. Known affectionately in Vietnam as Hai Ba Trung (the two sisters Trung), they succeeded in driving the Chinese governor and his security forces into Kwangtung. They proclaimed themselves queens of an independent kingdom and established their capital in Vinh Yen Province. Their rule was short lived, however, as a Chinese army defeated them in a battle at Lang Bac in A.D. 43. According to Vietnamese tradition, the Hai Ba Trung then committed suicide by drowning in the nearby Hat River. China subsequently reestablished direct rule.

Over the next 900 years, the indigenous leaders of Vietnam continued a pattern of resistance against their Chinese overlords. Although adopting Chinese culture and supporting Chinese administration as vassals in a feudal society, they seized the opportunities presented when Chinese dynasties were weak to reassert the independence of their ancestors. Over time, Chinese administrators who remained in Vietnam frequently adopted a similar attitude, viewing themselves less as representatives of the imperial court and more as leaders of an autonomous province. The period was marked by over a dozen major revolts.

One of the most famous of these was led by Trieu Au, a young Vietnamese woman from northern Vietnam. In A.D. 148, while riding on an elephant, Trieu Au led a small army of insurgents into battle. Although scoring many victories, she was ultimately defeated in much the same fashion as the Hai Ba Trung a century earlier. Trieu Au is a heroic figure in Vietnamese history, well-known for her stance on independence: "I want to rail against the wind and tide, kill the whales in the ocean, sweep the whole country to save my people from slavery, and I never accept to be the slave of anybody."[11]

During the long years of Chinese rule, numerous Vietnamese patriots followed the path of Trieu Au and the Trung sisters. In 468 Ly Truong Nhan revolted, slaughtered numerous Chinese officers, and proclaimed himself governor of the kingdom, then known as Chiao Chao, until China reasserted control. In 541 Ly Bon revolted and in

544 proclaimed himself emperor of Nam Viet, which he ruled for three years before the Chinese drove him into Laos, where he was killed. Although ethnically Chinese, Ly Bon is remembered as the first king of Vietnam and one of the great leaders of Vietnam's historic struggle for independence.[12] Ly Bon was followed by his lieutenant, Trieu Quang Phuc, who specialized in guerrilla warfare characteristic of latter-day Vietnam, and who secured, for a short time, control of the Red River valley.

Reestablishing control, Peking renamed its southern province "Annam," meaning "the Pacified South." This was an insult to the Vietnamese, who remained anything but pacified. Although the powerful T'ang dynasty exerted strong control over the area, nationalist revolts broke out in 687, 722, 766–791, and 819.[13] The Chinese suppressed all these revolts, putting to death the lords who led them and imposing even heavier taxation and labor burdens on the population that supported them.[14]

A principal reason for the failure of these revolts was that the Vietnamese lords who led them failed to mobilize the population into a people's war characteristic of twentieth-century Vietnam. Local mandarins led the revolts because their economic and political power was being eroded. Although favoring independence, most Vietnamese did not engage in armed rebellion. This situation changed by the beginning of the tenth century, as Joseph Buttinger clearly explains:

> The interests and aspirations that sparked the revolt of the upper classes against the Chinese at the same time estranged them from the mass of the people, the peasants who had resisted Sinicization. The hostility of the peasants, on the other hand, was directed primarily against the local upper class, which, though Chinese trained, was nevertheless the pioneer of national independence. Not until the ninth century did these conflicting trends begin to converge. . . . The upper class now made the peasants aware of the connection between national interest and their needs and harnessed their forces for action against the Chinese. The upper classes ceased to look at the peasant merely as an object of exploitation and began to look at him as an indispensable ally in their fight for independence. They mobilized the peasants by appealing to their common interests, and they stressed

those factors, which separated both of them from the Chinese. They began to speak the language of the villagers and to honor the peasant's pre-Chinese customs.[15]

Two other factors converged in the ninth century to make independence for Vietnam a realistic possibility. First was the decline of the T'ang dynasty. The dynasty collapsed in 907 and a period of instability ensued in China. Second, the threat from Champa subsided, in no small measure because of Chinese attacks on Vietnam's aggressive southern neighbor. (See map 3-2.)

Champa began as an independent state in about A.D. 192. A maritime people with a love for raiding coastal areas, the Cham (known earlier as the Lin Yi), joined with the Indianized kingdom of Funan (modern Cambodia and the present-day Mekong Delta) to pillage the towns of northern Vietnam. As the Cham tried to expand northward into lands of Chinese control, the Middle Kingdom reacted with strength.

> The fall of the Chin dynasty at the beginning of the fifth century led to such a spate of Cham attacks on Tongking that the Chinese governor was forced to appeal to the Imperial Court for help. In 431 the Chinese made a sea attack on Champa, but were driven off. It was in consequence of this threat that King Yang Mah [of Champa] tried, without success . . . to obtain the help of Funan in an attack on Tongking. In 446 a new Governor of Tongking, T'an Ho-ch'u, decided to teach the Lin-yi a severe lesson. He swooped down on their capital in the Hue region, plundered it and retired with a booty estimated at 100,000 lb. of pure gold. China, it is to be noted, made no attempt permanently to occupy and annex Lin-yi territory. Her aim was simply to keep her frontier region quiet by administering a dose of frightfulness to the "barbarians" beyond it. After this there was a long period of peace during which the customary embassies were sent to China.[16]

In 534 the king of Champa was granted investiture by China and sent an embassy to Peking (now Beijing). However, a few years later it again raided its Vietnamese neighbor, including attacks against Ly Bon, who was then in revolt against China. Chinese armies reacted by

Map 3.2. Dai Viet and Champa, A.D. 1350

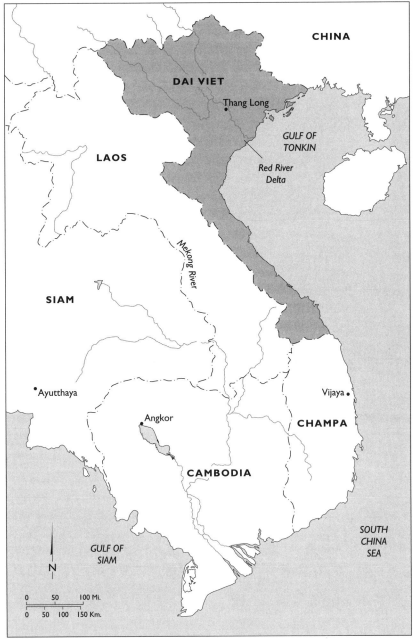

Bill Nelson

again invading and looting the Champa capital, but Champa neglected the annual tribute until the accession of the T'ang in 618.[17] As early as the seventh century, Vietnamese armies began to bash northern Champa.[18] By the tenth century, after the fall of the T'ang dynasty, Champa was generally on the defensive. Vietnam's Nam Tien (southward advance) had begun in earnest with slow but steady advances of Vietnamese farmers and villagers to the south. So, while China's punitive attacks on Champa helped maintain its southern Vietnamese province, they also eliminated a threat to its province of Annam and thereby contributed to its ability to focus on independence.

In Vietnam (Annam), meanwhile, popular antipathy for China continued and the independence movement gained momentum. "To the Vietnamese peasant, Chinese domination brought nothing but trouble. After the Ch'in, the Han, and then the Wu, during the Three Kingdoms period, they were again under the Wei, the Chin, the Sung, the Ch'i, and the Liang. Each of these dynasties had its own dictates, but the common denominator, except in a few instances, was despotic exploitation."[19]

By the tenth century, conditions for a successful revolt were manifest: a Chinese court in confusion, a reduced fear from attack by Champa, and a disgruntled peasantry allied with the Vietnamese mandarin class. All that was needed was a strong leader.

Independence

In 938 that leader arose in the person of Ngo Quyen. A native of Son Tay Province, Ngo came from a family dedicated to Vietnamese independence. His uncle, Duong Dien Nghe, had successfully defeated a Chinese army in 931 to win recognition as governor. Nghe thereupon began efforts to drive the Chinese from Vietnam, but in 937 was assassinated by Kieu Cong Tien, who strove to reestablish Chinese policies and rule. When Ngo Quyen took up arms against him, Kieu Cong Tran appealed to China for military intervention. A large Chinese army was sent down the Bach Dang River to teach Ngo Quyen a lesson.[20] As was the case in this incident and so often in subsequent Vietnamese history, the lesson taught was the other way around. Ngo Quyen had his men drive stakes into the riverbed at low tide, and when the Chinese fleet approached at high tide, he held them in position until the river once again receded, leaving the Chinese fleet impaled on the stakes. Ngo's victory was so complete that the following year he was able to proclaim himself the king of an independent Vietnam, which he called Giao Chi.[21]

The new kingdom, however, never controlled the Vietnamese chieftains (local warlords) and did not get Chinese recognition. A century of civil war ensued, known in Vietnam as the "Anarchy of the 12 Warlords," but the Sung dynasty was too weak to take advantage of it. In 968 Dinh Bo Linh united the 12 to form Dai Co Viet, and although independent, initiated the practice of Vietnamese leaders for nearly a thousand years of paying tribute to the Chinese, in large part to keep them at bay.[22]

The ensuing years saw Vietnamese both defeating Chinese armies in the field and paying tribute to Peking while the Chinese tried to turn that tribute into direct domination. In 980 Le Hoan defeated the Chinese at the Bach Dang River in much the same manner as Ngo Quyen had done earlier. In 1076 Vietnamese armies preempted a Chinese attack by invading southern China, inflicting heavy losses on the Chinese.[23] The Sung dynasty at the time was weak, having lost North China, but by the thirteenth century, the Mongol Yuan dynasty dominated China. Kublai Khan demanded Vietnam's submission, and out of fear, Tran Thanh Tong, who ruled from 1258 to 1278, provided not just triennial tribute, but also skilled craftsmen, scholars, and workers and accepted a "high censor" who monitored Vietnamese activity.[24] All this, however, was not enough for the Great Khan, who tried to absorb the kingdom by sending a Chinese-trained Vietnamese prince, Tran Di Ai, back to Vietnam with the title of "king of Annam." A Vietnamese army captured Ai at the border and sent the Chinese ambassador back with an arrow in his eye. This action prompted the khan to invade Vietnam with an army of 500,000 men.[25]

The Vietnamese are proud of their defeat of the Mongol army. Although initially penetrating deep into northern Vietnam, even butchering the population of the capital at Thanh Long (Hanoi), the Mongols found the weather and swamps of Vietnam difficult and started pulling back. Seizing the moment, the Vietnamese went on the offensive, and with their arms tattooed with the phrase "Death to the Mongols," devastated the invaders in a series of battles that followed. In 1285 the famous Vietnamese general Tran Hung Dao crushed the Mongols at the Battle of Bach Dang River, again using stakes to impale the Chinese fleet. The following year the Vietnamese ruler, Tran Nhan Tong, sent a delegation to the khan to renew tribute. Although the khan wanted to take reprisals for the Chinese defeat, he died before mobilizing the necessary forces, giving Vietnam a period of relative peace with its northern neighbor.[26]

Although it retained independence from China, Vietnam nonetheless continued to absorb aspects of Chinese culture. Buddhism was introduced primarily through China rather than through Southeast Asia.[27] By the ninth century, it reached all the way to Champa. After independence, Buddhist monks in Vietnam continued to transmit Chinese culture through their scholarly writings and teaching, and many attained high positions in the government.[28] Vietnam also retained many of the political institutions of China, including its administrative structure. In 1075 the Ly dynasty in Vietnam established mandarin exams in which Chinese learning was emphasized. Gradually, Confucian ideas spread. A Confucian temple of literature was established, and in the fourteenth century, Confucianism became widespread.[29] At the local level, the *Hat Bo* (Peking Opera) became very popular.

Unfortunately for Vietnam, this period of peace, during which the Tran dynasty ruled the country, witnessed increasing corruption and loss of governmental legitimacy during the fourteenth and fifteenth centuries. During this same period, the Ming dynasty in China was gaining strength and demanding an increased level of Vietnamese corvée labor and services.[30] At the outset of the fifteenth century, a government minister, Ho Quy Ly, reacted to general dissatisfaction with this situation by overthrowing the discredited Tran and reasserting Vietnamese culture. He promoted the use of Vietnamese script (the nom) to replace Chinese writing, denounced the Sung Golden Age, and condemned Confucianism. Loyalists to the Tran appealed to China for support, and in 1406 a large Chinese army descended on Vietnam, captured Ho Quy Ly, and established "the harshest foreign domination in the history of Vietnam."[31]

> Schools were permitted to teach only in Chinese. All local cults were suppressed. What national literature Vietnam had produced was confiscated and shipped to China. The women were forced to wear Chinese dress, the men to wear long hair; in order to tighten control of the people, an identity card was issued to every citizen. After ten years of Chinese rule, it was clear to every Vietnamese patriot that the survival of their people, more than ever before,

depended on their ability to free themselves from Chinese domination.[32]

As in the past, Vietnam found a leader to rescue the nation. A
landowner from Lam Son in central Vietnam, Le Loi, organized and
trained a local resistance movement that soon swept the country. Using
guerrilla tactics, he liberated areas of the countryside and recruited and
trained the liberated population to fight. With a motivated and trained
force, he defeated successive Chinese armies in the Red River delta and
in 1428 declared himself king of a dynasty that was to last, at least in
name, for 360 years.[33]

The Le dynasty is noteworthy for many achievements. With respect
to China, these included first the introduction of the Hong Duc Code
that lasted for centuries until replaced by the backward Chinese Gia
Long Code. Although a Confucianist, the great Vietnamese ruler Le
Thanh Tong established the Hong Duc Code as an integral part of
Vietnamese civil society that distinguished it from its northern neighbor.
The code established set rules of law, emphasized women's rights, and
included rules against abortion. Many Vietnamese today look to the
rule of Le Thanh Tong (1460–1497) as Vietnam's golden age.

A second achievement of the Le dynasty was a lessening of Vietnam's
dependence on China by the great Nam Tien (southward movement).
By the gradual movement of its people southward, moving from river
valley to river valley, Vietnam had been slicing off small parts of Champa
since the seventh century. Both sides fought occasional major battles,
but faced with the Mongol invasion of the thirteenth century, they
actually combined forces to defeat the invaders.[34] Nevertheless, as Vietnamese settlers continued encroaching on Cham territory, conflict appeared inevitable. The Cham appealed to China for protection, and
on several occasions a Chinese fleet did try to help. However, with rare
exceptions, Chinese naval power was not impressive, and in 1471 the
Le dynasty conquered Champa and absorbed it into the expanding
Vietnamese nation.[35] (See map 3-3.)

A Divided Vietnam

The de facto overthrow of the Le dynasty in the sixteenth century
further affected Sino-Vietnamese relations. When a court official, Mac
Dang Dung, overthrew the Le, he was not recognized by China, the

Map 3.3. Vietnam's Southward Expansion, 1000–1757

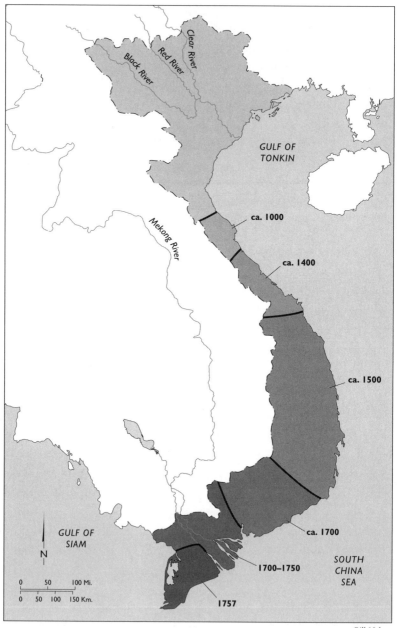

Bill Nelson

majority of leaders in northern Vietnam, or the Vietnamese of southern Vietnam. The Le family appealed to the Ming for restoration and under threat of Chinese invasion, Mac Dang Dung kowtowed to the Ming court for recognition, with tribute that included sending 40 Vietnamese dignitaries to China in chains.[36] In the name of restoring the Le dynasty, the Trinh family led a long struggle against the Mac and their Ming supporters. In 1592 the Trinh finally gained power in the north and thereafter ruled independently but claimed to represent the Le dynasty.[37]

The problem was that the ruling Nguyen family of southern Vietnam also claimed to represent the Le. In 1620 civil war broke out between the Trinh in the north and the Nguyen in the south. During the latter part of this struggle, the Trinh appealed to and received recognition from the new Ch'ing dynasty in China. The Nguyen, of course, received no such recognition, but welcomed Ming supporters who had fled from the Ch'ing.[38] In 1672, after over 50 years of conflict, the two sides finally agreed to peace.

During the century that followed (1672–1772), northern Vietnam remained under strong Chinese influence. The Trinh remained close to the Ch'ing and promoted Confucian learning. One of the Trinh rulers, Trinh Giang, sought to reduce Chinese influence by taxing Chinese merchants at higher rates, and by prohibiting the sale of Chinese books, but by and large the Trinh were careful not to irritate their northern neighbor.[39] The Chinese, at the same time, were not overanxious to invade Vietnam.

> Vietnam was enjoying relative peace. Although the Chinese would like to have resumed their domination, at that time Vietnam had reached a prominence that forced the respect of her neighbors. Its triumph over the Mongols, its conquest of Champa, its pacification of Laos, the glorious reign of Le Thai To (Le Loi), and the prestige of Le Thanh Tong were subjects of continual debate among Chinese politicians.[40]

The South under the Nguyen pursued an independent path without significant Chinese influence. Its geographic position allowed it to pursue its own interests without worrying about China's reaction. Those interests lay to the south and west. In 1672 the Nguyen took control of

Saigon (Prey Kor in Cambodian), in 1700 Ha Tien (on the southwestern periphery of modern Vietnam), and in the eighteenth century, the sparsely inhabited Mekong Delta. The South also pursued more vigorous international trade than the North, as the port of Fai Fo, near present-day Quang Nam Province, became a center for trade in silk and other commodities, with a significant overseas Chinese and Japanese presence. The Nguyen accommodated foreign merchants, including Westerners, and while generally hostile to the Christian faith, were more tolerant than the Trinh.[41] The Trinh, in contrast, patterned their reactions to the West after that of China, which generally meant isolation and lack of adaptation to change.[42]

Revolt and Unity

In the eighteenth century, the Nguyen court became increasingly arrogant and unconcerned about the welfare of the ordinary Vietnamese citizen. The court appointed Buddhist monks as princes and privileged officials, disassociating them from the people they were supposed to serve. Corruption became rampant and taxation oppressively high. The merchant class and foreigners were subject to abuse, and hopes for economic and political change were frustrated. When uncontrolled coin minting led to inflation and rice hoarding, famine stalked the land. In 1773 a revolt broke out, which was led by three brothers of Chinese descent from the village of Tay Son, near present-day An Khe. The revolt spread and the Tay Son rebels captured Saigon in 1776.[43]

The Tay Son faced not only decadence in the South, but also hostility in the North. Taking advantage of their revolt, the Trinh attacked and overcame the Tran Ninh wall dividing the two Vietnams at the Lien Giang River (near the 17th parallel that subsequently divided North and South Vietnam). The Tay Son reacted by conducting a successful guerrilla war. They also hired Cantonese mercenaries and soon gained control of central Vietnam. One of the brothers, the brilliant strategist Nguyen Hue, conquered the North, entered Thang Long (Hanoi) in 1786, and married the Le emperor's daughter. The emperor, however, mistrusted him and called for Chinese assistance. The Chinese responded by sending an army of 200,000 men under Sun Shih into Vietnam. Following a strategy to "lure them deep," Nguyen Hue retreated before the Chinese, who took Hanoi in 1789, but after a bitter battle outside the city, the Chinese army fled back to China. Le Chieu Thong, last ruler of the Le dynasty, later sought Chinese support, but they despised him.[44]

After defeating the Chinese, Nguyen Hue drafted a letter to the emperor Ch'ien Lung, who then agreed to recognize Nguyen Hue if he came to Peking to pay homage and to erect a statue to the slain Chinese warriors. Not trusting the Chinese, Nguyen Hue sent an envoy purporting to be himself to Peking to pay respect to the Chinese but no more. Hue then asked for control of Kwangsi and Kwangtung Provinces and refused to send gold statues, as was the customary tribute. Hue also made preparations to attack China if necessary.[45]

Tay Son rule, however, was short lived, as Nguyen Hue vied for leadership with his brother Nguyen Nhac, and the two did little to improve economic conditions in the country. In the ensuing vacuum of power, Nguyen Anh, the last surviving prince of the Nguyen dynasty of the South, seized control of all Vietnam. Aided by the French bishop, Pigneau de Behaine, he captured Saigon and returned power in the South to the Nguyen dynasty. In 1802, with the weakened North capitulating, he proclaimed himself the new emperor Gia Long and established his capital at Hue.[46]

Upon ascending the throne, Gia Long immediately dispatched an emissary to China, asking for formal investiture, which was granted in 1803 by the emperor Chia-Ching. The emperor stipulated that tribute must be sent every two years and homage performed every four years.[47] Gia Long faithfully observed these conditions throughout his reign.[48] He also followed China's policy of isolating itself from the West, rejecting modernization. He carried out the law of the Ch'ing as if Vietnam were a Chinese province, insisting on keeping China as the role model for Vietnam. He did not adhere to the traditional Vietnamese Hong Duc Code, but maintained the Confucian division of society.[49] He required conscription of males from 16 to 60 for corvée labor and military service as needed. Under his rule, "despite Western technological superiority the Vietnamese remained entrenched with the idea that China was the most powerful nation on earth and that Westerners were no better than the Mongolian barbarians."[50]

Successive Nguyen emperors of the united Vietnam continued Gia Long's policy.[51] Ming Mang, who reigned from 1820 to1840, and Tu Duc, who reigned from 1848 to 1883, were devout Confucianists and ardent admirers of things Chinese. Both persecuted Christians with unusual zeal, viewing missionaries as a threat to the Confucian tradition and in some cases political allies of their opponents. Tu Duc issued an edict of persecution requiring the words Ta Dao (infidel) to be burned on the cheeks of Christian people. According to at least one scholar, "There can be no doubt that Tu Duc took his cue from China and was too simple-minded to realize that the consequences for his country would be far more serious than those of the blustering Yeh's exhortations to exterminate the English devils for China. In 1856 a French Catholic missionary was tortured and killed for alleged complicity in rebellious society in Kwangsi province. . . . In 1857 Tu Duc had the Spanish Bishop of Tongking, Mgr. Diaz, put to death."[52]

Actions such as these invited French intervention, which had its own imperatives on the French side, but which now accelerated with considerable intensity.

The French Interlude

In 1857, having earlier secured Chinese government toleration of Catholics, the French gained extraterritorial rights in China by the Treaty of Tientsin. These French and other European "rights" in China were possible because of the relative backwardness and weakness of the Ch'ing dynasty. Nevertheless, without an effective policy for responding to the French, Tu Duc called for Chinese support and assistance. China responded by dispatching some troops from Yün-nan (Yunnan) Province. The ensuing struggle in northern Vietnam lasted until 1884, when the Chinese conceded French protectorate claims. Deprived of Chinese support, Vietnamese resistance weakened, and in 1887 France completed its campaign to gain control of Vietnam.[53] In that year France also secured from China rights to areas of the Gulf of Tonkin.[54] (See map 3-4.)

The French intervention in Indochina was an appendage to the overall European opening of China. With both commercial and religious motivation (the mix is a subject of debate), the French sought to establish themselves firmly in Vietnam while continuing to maintain "rights" in China. In the Treaty of Tientsin, France agreed to protect China's southern boundary, but in practice that meant commercial exploitation. For example, Frances Garnier, who later established himself as "the Great French Mandarin" in Hanoi, tried to open a trade route to the western provinces of China, first via the Mekong, and

Map 3.4. French Acquisitions in Indochina

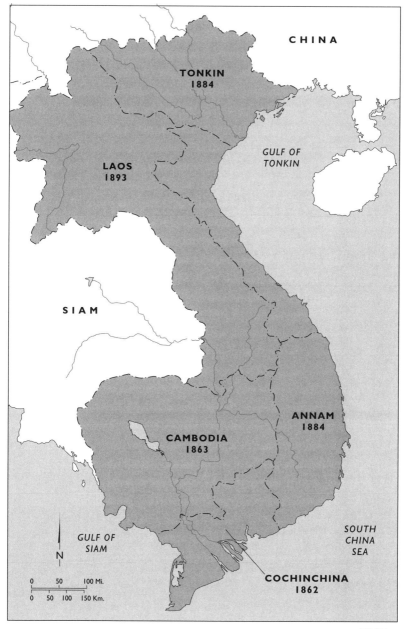

CHINA

TONKIN
1884

GULF OF
TONKIN

LAOS
1893

SIAM

ANNAM
1884

CAMBODIA
1863

GULF OF
SIAM

N

SOUTH
CHINA
SEA

COCHINCHINA
1862

0   50   100 Mi.

0   50   100   150 Km.

Bill Nelson

then via the Red River. After conspiring with a French merchant, Jean Dupuis, to bring arms and ammunition to a Chinese army in Yün-nan via the Red River, he tried to wrest control of the salt trade from the mandarins. As an indicator of things to come, both Garnier and the young Vietnamese emperor, Hiep Hoa, who had agreed to the French protectorate, were assassinated. In 1887 France formed the Union Indochinoise with a governor general.[55]

Official Sino-Vietnamese relations thereupon became part of Sino-French relations. However, as China was in such a weakened state, the real events that shaped the relationship were between nationalists in both China and Vietnam. While many Vietnamese nationalists placed their hopes in a movement to restore the emperor *(phong trao can vuong cuu quoc)*, others were influenced strongly by French philosophy as found in Montesquieu and Rousseau, and also by the contemporary Chinese reformer K'ang Yu-wei. In 1898 K'ang submitted a plan to the emperor for reform based on the study of Western culture. Such ideas appealed to nationalists who believed modernization would lead to independence. Among these was Phan Boi Chau, who turned first to Japan and then to China for ideas and support. Chau was strongly influenced by the Chinese revolution under the leadership of Sun Yat-sen, whom he met in Canton, where in 1912 Chau founded the Association for the Restoration of Vietnam, a revolutionary group dedicated to independence.[56]

A third group, the Constitutionalists, tried to get France to agree to reform, but the French, whose administration reached down even to local levels, repeatedly refused to transfer any real power to them. Frustrated, many Vietnamese turned to the Vietnam Quoc Dan Dang (Vietnam Nationalist Party), founded in 1927 with the support of the Nationalist Chinese party, the Kuomintang. The party initiated some terrorist activity and participated in an aborted rebellion in Yen Bay in 1930. Suppressed by the French, its core members fled to Yün-nan.[57]

Finally, a small number of Vietnamese activists turned to the Communists for leadership. In 1925 Ho Chi Minh (at the time under the alias Nguyen Ai Quoc) founded the Association of Revolutionary Vietnamese Youth in Canton (Thanh Nien), mostly of Vietnamese cadets trained at the Whampoa military academy by Borodin, the Russian Comintern agent. Merging with several other revolutionary groups, the Thanh Nien later changed its name to the Vietnam Communist Party. In 1930 Ho moved the organization to Haiphong and renamed it the Indochinese Communist Party. During the 1930s, Ho expanded his underground contacts in south China, and in late 1939 moved the Indochinese Communist Party to China for safety. As Japanese troops advanced southward, Chinese generals in south China sought an alliance with him, but Ho only agreed after languishing in prison for not collaborating with them.

In May 1941 Ho founded the Viet Nam Doc Lap Dong Minh Hoi (League for the Independence of Vietnam, abbreviated Viet Minh) in Kwangsi. Ostensibly an umbrella organization of Vietnamese nationalists, the organization received the support of Chinese nationalists in Chungking (Chongqing), and, during the last years of the war with Japan, from the U.S. Office of Strategic Services.[58]

Before arriving in Indochina, the Japanese arranged with the Vichy government for continuance of French rule in Indochina in exchange for military base and transit rights in that country. After arriving, however, they at best tolerated French rule, and in March 1945 the French leaders and military personnel were arrested. Japanese power in Vietnam subsequently dwindled, and by mid-1945 was quite weak. In August, knowing that the Potsdam Conference of the previous month stipulated that the British were to occupy southern Vietnam, and China the northern half of the country down to the 16th parallel, Ho took advantage of the power vacuum by proclaiming himself president of an independent Democratic Republic of Vietnam before the occupying forces arrived.[59] When the Chinese Nationalist occupation troops arrived, they pillaged the countryside and refused to let the French back into northern Vietnam until February 1946. Although this delay allowed Ho time to strengthen his party organization, his power at the time was quite limited. However, it increased substantially when the Chinese, who supported his opponents in the Vietnamese Nationalist Party and the Vietnamese Revolutionary Party, withdrew from Vietnam.[60]

Ho thereupon continued to consolidate power in the North but was unable to do so in the South, where released French prisoners and new contingents of French troops seized power in most key areas. Fearing the large-scale reintroduction of French troops into the North, Ho agreed to allow a token force of French troops to enter the North in exchange for French recognition of the Democratic Republic of

Vietnam with its own army. The French, however, increased their presence in the North as they attempted to reassert their sovereignty over all of Indochina. In the ensuing months, tensions escalated, and by November 1946 the First Indochina War had begun. During the first three years of that war, the government of Chiang Kai-shek was too absorbed in its own civil war to pay much attention to Vietnam. Under these conditions, the French held their own in the conflict and were able to control major population centers.

All that changed in 1949 when Mao Zedong seized power in Beijing. That year marked a definite shift in the military balance, as Chinese support for the Viet Minh dramatically increased. Whereas Chinese support for Vietnamese revolutionaries during the first half of the twentieth century provided a base from which Vietnamese leaders of different persuasions drew ideas and refuge, such support fell far short of that needed for a successful independence movement. That support materialized in a significant way only in 1950, when Chinese arms and ammunition assisted Viet Minh forces along the border in their drive to evict the French from Cao Bang and Lang Son. That same year China recognized the Democratic Republic of Vietnam (the government supported by the Viet Minh). During the ensuing years, Chinese arms and ammunition continued to flow to the Viet Minh in increasing quantities, as China became the "great rear base" for Viet Minh activity. By 1954 China was providing artillery pieces and 1,500 tons of supplies a month to Ho's forces, culminating in the vast artillery barrages that enabled the Viet Minh to overwhelm the French at Dien Bien Phu.[61]

The Chinese, however, appeared more interested in evicting the French and thereby creating a friendly state on their southern border than they were in the independence of Vietnam. During the Geneva talks that ended the First Indochina War, Chinese premier Zhou Enlai confided to French prime minister Pierre Mendès-France his position on the partitioning of Vietnam:

> Ho is getting too big for his britches. He does not listen to us . . . even after all that we have done for him. He listens too much, we think, to the Russians. So this is what we propose. Indochina should be cut into four zones. Ho will be allowed to keep North Vietnam, of course. But Laos and Cambodia should stay independent . . . and

continue as members of your French Overseas Union. The South of Vietnam should be partitioned off. A separate government could be formed there. We could talk of eventual unification by elections . . . but China would not mind if this unification did not actually occur.[62]

Although Vietnamese leaders later claimed to have been sold out at Geneva by Zhou, Ho nevertheless followed the Chinese path of communization, leading to the disastrous land reform programs of 1955 and 1956. Faced with peasant unrest and rebellion, Ho wound up begging China for aid, both food to avert rebellion and starvation, and military supplies to help "avert rebellion" and support his ambition to unite all Vietnam under his control.[63]

It was under these conditions that U.S. involvement in South Vietnam began, and so it is at this point that the significance of Sino-Vietnamese relations needs exposition and analysis.

Recurring Themes in Sino-Vietnamese Relations

Perhaps the most significant aspect of the over 2,000-year history of Sino-Vietnamese relations is the dichotomy between the importance of China to Vietnam and the reverse. For China, Vietnam was relatively insignificant. It was a land with a much smaller population, and one that China controlled as a province for over a thousand years. After Vietnam became independent, it still paid tribute to the Middle Kingdom, and if it did not, China would send an army to teach it a lesson. The relationship was an unequal one, with the king of Vietnam requiring investiture by the Chinese emperor, and the court of Vietnam paying tribute, usually on a triennial basis, to the imperial Chinese court. The attitude of the Chinese rulers toward their southern neighbor was one of superiority, referring to them at various times in history as Nan Yueh (southern barbarians), and the kingdom of Annam (the Pacified South, implying a defeated or conquered South).

China, in contrast, was of vital importance to Vietnam. China was the dominant civilization in the region, one that absorbed and Sinicized numerous other peoples as it expanded over time. The southward movement of Chinese people and culture threatened and almost succeeded in doing the same to Vietnam. Even the French term "Indo-chinese" bespeaks the degree of Chinese influence they saw in the region. Vietnamese fear of being overwhelmed by the colossus to the north thus drove the people of Vietnam to extraordinary lengths to define themselves as a separate people and nation. Stories of Vietnam's prehistorical legends of Van Lang and of the historical kingdom of Nam Viet imbued into the consciousness of the people of the Red River valley a sense of separate identity. Likewise, the culture of Vietnamese society favored a separate national identity. Although absorbing a multitude of Chinese characteristics over the millennia, it retained a distinctiveness perhaps best represented by the Hong Duc Code, with its respect for women and the duties and rights of individuals. Vietnam's effort to retain its own political and cultural identity is, at the heart, an effort to maintain its existence as a people and a nation—the struggle for independence.

The Pattern of the Relationship

As Vietnam struggled for its precious independence and China sought to maintain its role as the dominant political and cultural center of Asia, a pattern developed in their relationship that repeated itself with minor variations for over 2,000 years. The essential outlines of that pattern is as follows:

1. Chinese pressure on Vietnam
2. Vietnamese Sinicization and accommodation
3. Tyranny and rebellion in Vietnam
4. Civil war in which China intervenes to support the old regime, followed by Vietnamese military victory
5. Vietnamese tribute, reconciliation, and eventual regime corruption
6. Renewed Chinese pressure

1. Chinese Pressure on Vietnam

Throughout history, the combination of a powerful China and a weak Vietnam typically threatened the independence of Vietnam, while a weakened China and a strong Vietnam had the reverse effect. It is no accident that the first Vietnamese historical state, Nam Viet, attained independence upon the fall of the Ch'in dynasty and that a hundred years later that kingdom was conquered by the increasing power of the great Han dynasty. The revolt by Ly Truong Nhan occurred at the end of the eastern Chin dynasty, and Cham attacks on the Chinese province in northern Vietnam at the beginning of fifth century occurred upon the fall of the eastern Chin. The new and powerful T'ang dynasty ruled Annam with an iron hand until, as it began to decline in the ninth century, it began to lose control. With the collapse of the T'ang in 907, the Vietnamese independence movement gained momentum and in 938 ended the thousand-year Chinese rule, a rule that was reimposed temporarily only in the fifteenth century by the then-powerful Ming dynasty.

It is no less true that Vietnamese independence was also a function of its own internal strength and weakness. When Vietnam was strong, with a united population, it withstood even strong Chinese dynasties. When it was weak, it invited trouble. Thus the unity of effort by the people and the mandarins, supported even by the Cham, led to victory over the powerful Mongol armies of Kublai Khan. But when in the fifteenth century, palace extravagance paid for by heavy taxes led to destitution and popular revolts against the Tran dynasty, the Chinese took advantage of the situation to impose direct rule.

2. Sinicization and Accommodation

The Sinicization of Vietnam brought many benefits. Economically it fostered greater agricultural productivity through the use of tools and the *don dien* (fort, rice field) system that provided army veterans plots of land on the frontier. The Vietnamese copied this system from the Chinese and used it to push their frontiers southward.[64] Politically, the Chinese introduced an administrative system that helped organize society and increase overall national wealth. Culturally, it introduced Buddhism and Confucian thought, as well as language and arts. Moreover, numerous Vietnamese patriots, such as Ly Bon and the Tay Son brothers, were of Chinese descent.

But Sinicization also challenged the fabric of Vietnamese independence. It catered to the elite in Vietnam, created an examination system to the mandarinate based on knowledge of Confucianism and the Chinese classics, fostered Chinese writing for official correspondence and documents, and promoted elite intermarriage with Chinese dignitaries. It also included attempts to alter the personal customs of ordinary Vietnamese in areas such as dress and hair style, and imposed heavy and often harsh tax burdens on the peasantry.

The dichotomy between the reaction of the mandarins and the peasantry to Sinicization is most interesting. The mandarins were by far the most Sinicized. During the thousand years of Chinese rule, their power depended on good relations with their Chinese overlords, and they became more and more Chinese in their culture. Even after independence, they continued to focus their study on the Chinese classics; adopted Chinese customs; and in many cases, turned to China for support against peasant rebellion. The ordinary Vietnamese, however, resisted Sinicization. Many of them developed a hostile attitude toward the mandarins, viewing them as agents of Chinese rule.[65] They maintained their own village language and performed their duties such as corvée labor when necessary, but they resisted further impositions of Chinese rule and culture at the village and farm level.

3. Tyranny and Rebellion

Chinese rule, either directly for the first millennium of the modern era or indirectly through the mandarins, exploited the average Vietnamese and at various times threatened the power of the mandarins. These conditions strengthened the Vietnamese desire for independence, leading to revolts throughout the long centuries of Chinese rule and armed resistance to subsequent Chinese attempts to control Vietnam. Great Vietnamese rebel leaders, such as the Hai Ba Trung of the first century, Ba Trieu of the third century, and Ly Bon of the sixth century, were not, however, successful in gaining permanent independence for their native land. That accomplishment came only when the mandarins allied with the population at large to form a true people's army in the tenth century under Ngo Quyen. Popular support was also crucial in Tran Hung Dao's defeat of the Mongols in 1285, in Le Loi's successful guerrilla war from 1418 to 1427 to free Vietnam from Chinese rule, and in Nguyen Hue's Tay Son rebellion that drove an invading Chinese army back into China.

4. Civil War and Vietnamese Military Victory

Vietnamese rebellion, either by the mandarins or a broader segment of the population, typically meant the overthrow of an existing regime that had become corrupt and oppressive. Such regimes did not cede power easily, and the ensuing struggle frequently witnessed the old regime appealing to China for military support. If the rebels had the support of the people, they in turn typically crushed the Chinese army and seized power.

Thus in 937 Kieu Cong Tien sought to represent Chinese power and killed the Vietnamese patriot Duong Dinh Nghe, only to be faced with a popular revolt led by Ngo Quyen. When a Chinese army came to Kieu Cong Tien's support, Ngo Quyen defeated him to gain Vietnamese independence. In 1406 loyalists to the corrupt Tran called for and received Chinese support against the rebel Ho Quy Ly, leading to 20 years of the harshest rule Vietnam ever experienced. After the military victories of Le Loi liberated the country, the Le dynasty went into a slow decline, leading to revolution in the sixteenth century. The warlord Mac Dang Dung kowtowed to the Ming, murdered the Vietnamese patriot Nguyen Kim, and appealed for Chinese assistance against his Trinh descendants. Again the Chinese were defeated in battle. Finally, in the Tay Son rebellion of the late eighteenth century, the figurehead king Le Chieu, taking advantage of Nguyen Hue's absence in his struggle against the southern Nguyen, invited a Chinese army in to restore his crown. When the Chinese treated Vietnam as conquered territory, Nguyen Hue gained greater Vietnamese support and defeated the Chinese by attacking them during the celebration of Tet (the Oriental New Year) in 1789.[66]

These are but a few of the illustrations of Vietnamese revolution and civil strife, in which collaborators with China (also known as Viet gian, or traitors) appealed to China to support their power against their own people. Throughout history it was primarily the unity of the people and the military capabilities of its leaders that saved the nation from Chinese domination. Vietnam supplemented this effort by "keeping the emperor at bay" through regular tribute.

5. Tribute, Reconciliation, and Eventual Regime Corruption

Because of its relative strength upon gaining independence in 938, Vietnam did not immediately begin paying tribute to the Chinese imperial court. Vietnam soon realized, however, that China demanded payment of the tribute. Thus in 968 Vietnam began paying tribute, usually every three years, for nearly a thousand years. In addition, Vietnamese kings sought investiture by the Chinese emperor before assuming the throne.

One of the most important aspects of the tribute was that the payment was sent immediately after Vietnamese military victories. Having defeated "the great Han," Vietnamese rulers sought to assuage Chinese pride by respectfully offering generous gifts. Le Loi offered the Chinese army he had just defeated provisions to return home. A year after nearly destroying the Mongol invaders, Tran Hung Dao offered tribute to Kublai Khan. Nguyen Hue, having utterly defeated a Chinese army, pledged fealty to the Chinese emperor and erected statues to the Chinese warriors he had slain. These and other acts of Vietnamese deference to the Chinese court reconciled Vietnam with China for a time and permitted a period of peace that Vietnam so badly needed. Unfortunately for Vietnam, however, its dynasties assumed power without the checks and balances needed for the long-term welfare of its people, and successive Vietnamese rulers eventually became corrupt, kowtowing to the Chinese and laying increasing burdens on the people.

6. Popular Discontent and Renewed Chinese Pressure
The increasing corruption of the leadership and its increasing dependence on China then led to discontent among the population, prompting a new set of Vietnamese patriots to arise and renewed Chinese pressure, and the cyclical nature of Vietnamese history began all over again.

Breaking the Cycle of History
Throughout its long history, Vietnamese deference to China had three advantages. The first was protection against outside invaders. In ancient times Chinese armies attacked and plundered Champa when that kingdom threatened the Chinese state of Giao Chi in the Red River valley. In modern times, Chinese assistance was important to the success of the Democratic Republic of Vietnam, first against the French and then against the United States.[67] The second advantage was the organizational and practical skills brought by Sinicization. At a time when Vietnam's international contacts were extremely limited, Chinese culture helped modernize the society to a certain extent. The third advantage was protection from China itself. The tribute given and the investiture of kings requested demonstrated that Vietnam recognized the superiority of the Middle Kingdom, thereby "keeping China at bay."

These advantages, however, were of limited value during the long history of Vietnam, and may be even more so in the Vietnam of the twenty-first century. First, Chinese protection against outside powers was a temporary phenomenon. Chinese protection against the Cham was limited to a few punitive attacks while Vietnam was under Chinese domination. By the ninth century, Vietnam was in the ascendancy, and by the fifteenth century, it had conquered Champa. So too, in the long scope of Vietnamese history, Chinese assistance against the French was but a temporary phenomenon. Although that assistance definitely helped, on more than one occasion China sold out Vietnam when their interests conflicted. When looking at the twenty-first century, it is difficult to imagine that Chinese "protection" will be needed against any country. Certainly the Japanese, the French, and the Americans have no interest in returning to Vietnam with military force any time in the foreseeable future, and Vietnam seems quite capable of defending itself against any likely threat that may eventuate from its Southeast Asian neighbors. The simple truth is that Vietnam does not need Chinese protection against any external threat, now or in the foreseeable future.

Second, Sinicization taught Vietnam more modern agricultural methods and ways to organize government to establish political order. However, the advantages of Sinicization were a mixed blessing. The stratification of society along Confucian lines, the alignment of the mandarins with Chinese thought and policy, often at the expense of the ordinary Vietnamese, and the vicious cycle of corruption by an elite not responsible to the people but to China, all harmed the development of Vietnamese independence and freedom. The psychological dependency manifested by Gia Long and his successors in following Chinese policy of isolation from the West and rejecting modernization was based on the idea that China was so powerful and Vietnam so weak that it must follow the Chinese path.[68] It is no accident that the Vietnamese elites of today, schooled in Marxist thought, look to China as a political and economic model in much the same way as their predecessors, schooled in the Chinese classics, did. Both elites perceive Vietnam as the student and China as the teacher. This psychological dependency by the elite is the antithesis of the independence and freedom for which ordinary Vietnamese have fought for centuries.

Finally, the idea of paying tribute so as not to provoke the emperor was crucial to Vietnam's survival at a time when China was the only major power in the region and controlled the international behavior of surrounding states. Yet even under these conditions China still sent armies into Vietnam to stifle revolts against corrupt mandarins who were compliant with the wishes of the emperor. Tribute to China did not extricate Vietnam from the vicious cycle of Chinese aggression—Sinicization and accommodation by the mandarins, followed by corruption and tyranny, rebellion and civil war, Vietnamese military victory, tribute, and eventual corruption leading to further rebellion and Chinese aggression. To break this cycle, Vietnam needed to look in a different direction from China. The southward movement of Vietnamese peoples (the Nam Tien) did just that. It moved Vietnam away from its heavy dependence on China and brought it into contact with other cultures. So too as it advances in the twenty-first century, Vietnam needs to recognize that the world has changed, and that while China remains close and powerful, Vietnam's interests in a multipolar world lie in a balanced and independent foreign policy that kowtows to no emperor.

CHAPTER 4

Land Border and South China Sea Disputes

As China and Vietnam reached agreement on 25 December 2000 on demarcating the Gulf of Tonkin, both sides expressed optimism regarding the future of their relationship. With the striking of this agreement on sea boundaries in the wake of a land border agreement at the end of 1999, it appeared the two sides had reached accommodation with each other's national interests in these two zones of friction. In fact, however, the land border agreement was to some degree cosmetic, with significant obstacles remaining to be resolved, while Vietnam yielded its position on major claims in the Gulf of Tonkin with very little in the way of Chinese quid pro quo. More important, China and Vietnam continued to disagree over both ownership and the behavior of each other's commercial and military activities in the South China Sea.

These disagreements are the most obvious irritants in current Sino-Vietnamese relations and are focused on three major offshore areas—the Paracel Islands, the Spratly Islands, and the Con Son Basin. Each of these areas has its own set of problems—economic, political, and military—but they are also interrelated with the fabric of overall bilateral relations and the vision each nation has of its own maritime future. This chapter examines the nature of disputes in all five of these areas, and how those disputes are likely to affect future relations between the two neighbors.

Land Border

Although in the late 1970s both China and Vietnam complained of a large number of border incidents, Vietnamese leaders today say they do not perceive disputes over their common land border as an important factor in China's decision to attack Vietnam in 1979. Along the entire 797-mile border China claimed fewer than 60 square kilometers of Vietnamese-held territory.[1] The Vietnamese claim that the border area had enjoyed a long period of peace and that ethnic groups on both sides of the border had a close relationship. The border, an interviewed Vietnamese military officer said, had not been a major problem before they unified the country in 1975:

> Historically, the border was always amorphous. Vietnam was a tributary state, but independent for many years, similar to the Finland/ Russia relationship—a zone of security and influence. With the rise of the People's Republic of China, Beijing sought to reassert sovereignty of the great Han—a zone of security and influence similar to that which they enjoyed in North Korea, where China entered the war with the USA to protect that zone. But at least the Democratic Republic of Vietnam remained free as such a zone. This worked to our advantage during the war with the United States.[2]

How, then, did the border conflict arise? Clearly, there was a real difference of views on interpretation of the 1887 Franco-Chinese border demarcation agreement. Drawn on a map at the time, the agreed border became more concrete at the turn of the century when a total of 333 border markers were laid. However, these markers were not well maintained over the years, and after unifying the country in 1975, Hanoi charged that some of them had been moved south. Leaders in Hanoi said they had been too preoccupied with their various wars to focus on the markers and that throughout the wars with France and the United States, the PRC had told them that the land border was not a problem and could be settled later. The same applied to demarcation issues in the Gulf of Tonkin.[3]

The differences in interpretation took on greater significance in the 1970s. According to the Vietnamese view, as expressed by a former Vietnamese diplomat, "as Chinese strategic interests shifted in the 1970s and 1980s, it posited new demands on land and at sea. Beijing said it had to 'stabilize the border to make Chinese territory safe for development.' China charged Vietnam was attacking China, but Vietnam could never attack and occupy China."[4] Other sources cite Hanoi as becoming unduly provocative in the wake of its victory over Saigon. Vietnam made claims beyond the border delimited in the Sino-French agreement and began raising the issue of a "historical" borderline to support claims to 15 separate pieces of land in Yunnan and Guangxi Provinces.[5] "We made mistakes in our attitude toward China," a Vietnamese foreign ministry official admitted.[6] The mistakes clearly irritated the Chinese, adding fuel to the other causes of the 1979 border war.

On 17 February 1979, the People's Liberation Army (PLA) crossed the border with Vietnam, intent on teaching Vietnam a lesson. The principal causes of the conflict were Vietnam's quasi alliance with the Soviet Union, dubbed the "hegemonist" by China; Vietnam's attack on Cambodia, which China viewed as part of its sphere of influence; and Vietnam's expulsion of many of its ethnic Chinese Hoa people. Land and South China Sea border issues played a secondary role.

Although People's Army of Vietnam (PAVN) troops taught the PLA a military lesson, China taught Vietnam a political lesson. First, it taught Vietnamese leaders that China would not hesitate to use force in the event Vietnamese interests seriously conflicted with those of China. Second, it contributed to Vietnam's strategic isolation in world affairs. While China was able to build bridges to the international community, Vietnam was left holding the bag of international opprobrium for its occupation of Cambodia. Third, Chinese artillery and patrol activity inside Vietnam, which continued long after the Chinese withdrawal in March 1979, forced Vietnam to maintain a large military force oriented toward China and inhibited its campaign against the Khmer Rouge in Cambodia. Together with regressive economic policies, this led to further deterioration of Vietnam's weak economy. Only with the evacuation of PAVN troops from Cambodia in the late 1980s, and the concurrent demise of the Soviet empire, did China and Vietnam initiate the process of normalization of relations.[7]

In January 1989 Hanoi and Beijing held discussions on ways to improve bilateral relations at the deputy foreign minister level. In September 1990 Chinese and Vietnamese leaders met secretly at Chengdu, China, to discuss normalization. In November 1991 the Vietnamese general secretary and foreign minister went to Beijing. The leaders of the two countries agreed to put the past behind them and to look to the future, declaring that they would improve and normalize relations in conformity to the interests of both peoples and promote peace, cooperation, and development.[8]

In these discussions the two sides agreed to settle the land border as a prelude to dealing with other territorial disputes. Official talks specifically focusing on land border issues began in 1993. Expert-level talks began the following year, and in 1996 the railway connecting Guangxi, China, to Lang Son, Vietnam, reopened. In July 1997 Vietnamese Communist Party secretary-general Do Muoi met with his Chinese counterpart, Jiang Zemin, in Beijing. The two leaders agreed to settle the land border dispute before the year 2000.[9] Another positive sign indicating a possible border settlement was the PLA effort of the late 1990s to clear land mines along the border. In August 1999 China announced that the PLA had completed this task, removing all 2.2 million mines from the border area.[10]

In 1999 China and Vietnam reached early agreement on the demarcation of 900 kilometers of their 1,350-kilometer common border. They claimed 289 areas were still in dispute along the remaining 450 kilometers. They divided these areas into three categories, as shown in the following table (table 4-1):

Table 4-1: Sino-Vietnamese Land Border Claims

Type	Number of areas of dispute	Total disputed area (square km)	Rationale for the dispute
A	74	unknown	different mapping techniques
B	51	5	technical errors
C	164	230 (60 unclear)	historical, control and management

Source: Dr. Tran Cong Truc, chairman of the Vietnamese Government Border Commission, "Official SRV-China Border Treaty," Hanoi *Tap Chi Quoc Phong Toan Dan*, 35–37, 1 February 2000.

The type A and type B disputes were resolved early in the negotiations. Type C disputes were more complicated. The negotiators divided this type into two categories, "clear" and "unclear." The "clear" disputes were those specifically identifiable as falling under the Sino-French border conventions of 1887 and 1895, and were resolved in accordance with them. The "unclear" disputes were the most difficult. They involved issues of the location of border markers, conflicting historical maps, current management and control, current or recent occupancy, terrain definition, and international law.

On 30 December 1999 China and Vietnam finally concluded an agreement. Both sides trumpeted the agreement as a final solution to their long-standing border problems. The Chinese foreign ministry stated that, "with the joint efforts of the two sides, the issue of the border between the two countries has been completely resolved."[11] The chairman of Vietnam's Border Commission, Dr. Tran Cong Truc, stated that "we have reached a complete solution for one of the most difficult problems left behind by history."[12]

The reality of the land border situation is somewhat different. Although great progress was made toward final resolution of bilateral problems, significant areas remain where negotiations have not produced agreement. According to Tran Cong Truc, the borderline still has to be defined in many areas and border markers put in place. Fieldwork still needs to be done, and both sides must sign a protocol to certify the maps and minutes in accordance with international law and customary practice, and then they must sign a convention on border management."[13] Although both sides ratified the agreement, the fact that further border talks were being held in 2000 is a clear indication that complete resolution of issues is not yet accomplished.[14] Another round of land border talks was held in February, and in April Vietnamese vice foreign minister Vu Khoan stopped in Beijing to discuss follow-up on the land border agreement, indicating that further arrangements still need to be made. According to the Vietnamese side, these arrangements may take "several years."[15]

South China Sea Disputes

There are many disputes over control of various parts of the South China Sea, but those between China and Vietnam are the most numerous and contentious. The two nations have finally reached agreement on demarcation of the Gulf of Tonkin, but they continue to have conflicting claims to three other areas of the sea: the Paracel Islands, the Spratly Islands, and the Con Son Basin. As shown in table 4-2, each country has given its own name to both the entire South China Sea and the

Table 4-2: Sino-Vietnamese Nomenclature for the South China Sea

English	Chinese	Vietnamese
South China Sea	Nanhai Zhudao	Truong Xa
Gulf of Tonkin	Beibu Wan	Bac Bo
Paracel Islands	Xisha Qundao	Quan Dao Hoang Xa
Spratly Islands	Nansha Qundao	Quan Dao Truong Xa
Con Son Basin	Wan-an Bei	Tu Chinh

four zones they have historically contested. Each of these four areas has its own historical, legal, political, and economic value to China and Vietnam. Each also has been the scene of clashes between the two over the past 30 years. Their disagreements may eventually be settled peacefully, but given the intractability of both sides in the most recent three years, the best option for the immediate future appears to lie in mutual acceptance of confidence-building measures that seek to both demilitarize the South China Sea and prevent incidents between rival claimants. This is the focus of current efforts within the Association of Southeast Asian Nations (ASEAN) and in Track II talks seeking to defuse conflict.

The Gulf of Tonkin

On 25 December 2000, the foreign ministers of China and Vietnam signed agreements on demarcation of and fishing in the Gulf of Tonkin. Both the "Agreement on the Demarcation of Waters, Exclusive Economic Zones, and Continental Shelves" and the "Agreement on Fishing Cooperation" offered the hope of resolving one of the greatest irritants in Sino-Vietnamese relations, and one that has the potential to provoke local conflict between Chinese and Vietnamese forces.[16] The two countries had conflicting claims in the gulf, and both demonstrated a willingness to support those claims by permitting, and even promoting, fishing and petroleum exploration in disputed areas. As a result, the Gulf of Tonkin became a zone of intense competition and a flash point that needed to be resolved if bilateral disputes in other areas of the South China Sea are to be attenuated.

The agreement was the culmination of nine years of intense negotiation during which China maintained a steadfast position on the demarcation issue while creating the expectation that an agreement had to be reached within a specified time period. The time element was first announced in the Do Muoi–Jiang Zemin summit of 1997, when both sides pledged to reach an agreement on maritime disputes in the Gulf of Tonkin in the year 2000. China subsequently reinforced this expectation in its press releases and meetings with Vietnamese leaders. Casting the agreement as part of an effort to "define the framework and development direction of bilateral relations to the 21st century," General Secretary Jiang Zemin reiterated his expectation of a 2000 settlement to his Vietnamese counterpart, Le Kha Phieu, in a February 1999 summit in Beijing.[17] Talks on the gulf continued in numerous sessions in 1999 and 2000, typically with the announced objective of accelerating negotiations in order to reach agreement by the end of 2000.[18] A fundamental disagreement on demarcation, however, complicated the hopes of meeting that deadline.

Vietnam claimed that the Gulf of Tonkin, which it calls Bac Bo, or the "Northern Gulf," is its historic waters. It claimed all resources and islands west of a line running directly south from its coastal border with China. (See map 4-1.) The claim was based on the 1887 Franco-Chinese Convention that fixed the frontier between French Indochina and China at 105 degrees and 43 minutes east of the Paris meridian, (108 degrees and 3 minutes east of Greenwich).[19] This delineation would have given Vietnam the lion's share of offshore resources in the gulf.

The Chinese disputed the Vietnamese claim, stating that China has had a historic presence in the gulf. A Chinese archeological team visiting the area in 1999, for example, claimed to have found 1,500 Chinese artifacts dating back a thousand years.[20] While the claim may be exaggerated, Chinese control of Vietnam before A.D. 938, and its continuing influence in surrounding areas ever since, makes at least part of the claim likely.

China reinforced its claims in the gulf by reference to the 1982 United Nations Convention on the Law of the Sea. It claimed that this law gave China legitimate rights over waters east of a median line between Hainan Island and the coast of northern Vietnam. Beijing referred to this area as a "territorial sea" of China. This equidistant

Map 4.1. Resources and Claims in the South China Sea

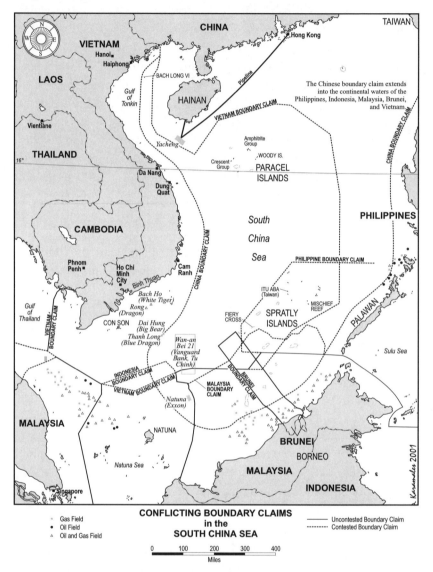

CONFLICTING BOUNDARY CLAIMS
in the
SOUTH CHINA SEA

Gas Field
Oil Field
Oil and Gas Field

Uncontested Boundary Claim
Contested Boundary Claim

0   100   200   300   400
Miles

line, based on a delimitation of respective continental shelves, dismisses Vietnam's argument that the Bach Long Vi, a Vietnamese islet some 54 nautical miles from the Vietnamese coast in the gulf, provides a legitimate rationale for extension of the demarcation line further to the east.

Although historic and legal rationales buttress China's claims to the gulf, its need for petroleum and the prospect of petroleum discoveries appear to impel recent Chinese actions. In 1994, for the first time in recent years, China began to be a net importer of oil. In 1999 it imported a record amount, 36.6 million tons, while Chinese oil production at 160 million tons declined for the first time in recent decades. In 2000 China's total demand for crude was over 200 million tons, of which over 50 million tons were imported.[21] Chinese imports of crude oil are expected to triple over the next decade. China realized its domestic energy supply could not meet projected demand. In the early 1990s, it began serious petroleum exploration in the northern end of the South China Sea. The China National Offshore Oil Corporation teamed up with Atlantic Richfield to exploit a very large gas field south of Hainan Island. In 1996 this Yacheng field began producing natural gas for China via underwater pipelines to Hainan and Hong Kong. With an estimated 85 billion cubic meters of recoverable gas, Yacheng has become the largest Chinese offshore gas field. China's success with the field, located only 100 nautical miles from the Vietnamese coast, whetted its appetite for petroleum in the nearby Gulf of Tonkin. It intensified its exploration activities in the gulf, at one time having as many as six rigs inside the zone claimed by Vietnam.

In March 1997 a Chinese oil rig began exploration some 60 nautical miles from Vietnam's coast and well within the Vietnamese-claimed line. Vietnam protested the Chinese action, but to no avail. It then appealed to other ASEAN countries, whose ambassadors in Hanoi responded by making statements supportive of Vietnam's position. In April the Chinese withdrew the rig but stated that it was a temporary withdrawal for technical reasons. An emergency meeting in Beijing between Vietnamese vice foreign minister Vu Khoan and Chinese foreign minister Qian Qichen failed to resolve the issue.[22] In 1998 officials of the Chinese National Offshore Oil Corporation and Petro-Vietnam began exchange visits, but no announced progress was made at that time.[23]

For its part, Vietnam did not stand still. In early 2000 Hanoi announced that it would initiate a new project in the Gulf of Tonkin through Vietsovpetrol, its joint venture with Russia that accounts for 80 percent of Vietnam's oil and gas production.[24] This follows by one month a production-sharing contract with American Technologies,

Inc., for exploration and exploitation of petroleum reserves at the northern end of the gulf within Vietnam's continental shelf.[25]

Another problem centered on fishing. Fishing boats from both sides assiduously exploited the marine reserves in the gulf, and there were numerous reports of minor conflicts between fishermen and constant apprehensions of the other side's fishermen by the coastal patrols of both governments. During the mid-1990s, for example, Vietnam reported a total of 5,371 cases of foreign violations of Vietnam's fishing grounds in the Tonkin Gulf. Without specifically identifying China as the violator, Vietnam clearly pointed to China, noting that "foreign fishing vessels operated under the support of war ships and when detected they attacked the Vietnamese coast guard ships and opened up ways for illegal fishing vessels to escape. Some of the warships even threatened Vietnamese fishing vessels in their own fishing ground."[26] Vietnam further charged that "foreign trawlers, chiefly from China, penetrated into Vietnamese fishing grounds to illegally catch aquatic products. . . . At night and when the sea is rough, they move close to the coast, even only 10 nautical miles off Nghe An [on the Gulf of Tonkin] and three nautical miles from Bach Long Vi Island. Some foreign trawlers even bear fake registration plates and carry Vietnamese flags to mix with Vietnamese trawlers operating in the fishing ground."[27]

Although charges and countercharges of fishing violations declined in the late 1990s in accordance with the policies of each government to emphasize the positive in their relationship, numerous reports of incidents continue. In July 1998 Vietnam reported apprehending 57 Chinese fishermen in the gulf.[28] In July 1999 China reported detaining seven Vietnamese fishing boats and driving away forty more that had violated its fishing areas in Beibu Wan. The incident was part of Chinese enforcement of its temporary ban on fishing in the South China Sea.[29]

Given the stakes involved, Beijing was most satisfied with the outcome of the bilateral negotiations on the gulf that concluded at the end of 2000. The final agreement gave China rights to ocean resources all the way to the median line between Hainan Island and the Vietnamese coast, a position Vietnam had opposed for historic, legal, and economic reasons throughout the negotiations. Bach Long Vi, the Vietnamese-held island in the gulf, was given no consideration in the demarcation, and with the exception of a small sector surrounding Vietnamese offshore islands in the northern end of the gulf, Vietnamese claims were rejected.[30] Thus the agreement, while reducing tensions in the Gulf of Tonkin, augurs poorly for equitable resolution of the three other areas of dispute in the South China Sea. This fact was driven home the very day of the agreement, when a spokeswoman for the Chinese foreign ministry announced, "China's position on the South China Sea is very clear, that China has indisputable sovereignty over the Spratly Islands and surrounding waters."[31]

The Paracel Islands

The Paracel Islands are the second area of Sino-Vietnamese disputes in the South China Sea. Lying some 250 nautical miles east of Da Nang, the Paracels consist of two island groups: the Amphitrite Group to the east and the Crescent Group to the west. The entire land area of the Paracels totals 7.6 square kilometers, the largest of which is Woody Island, with almost 2 square kilometers.[32]

China has multiple claims to the Paracel Islands. First, it argues that its claim is supported by the 1887 Sino-French convention. That agreement gave China the right to all islands east of the longitude both countries had agreed to in dividing the Gulf of Tonkin. While Vietnam holds that this convention pertained only to the Gulf of Tonkin, China interprets it as pertaining to all of the South China Sea. Second, it claims a historic presence in the islands as evidenced by artifacts and records of ship visits dating to the Han dynasty. China supports this argument by citing recent discoveries of Chinese pottery and other items in the area. Third, China points out that it was the first country to exercise sovereignty over the Paracels, citing a 1909 claim.[33]

Vietnam rejects all these positions. First, it holds that the 1887 Sino-French convention was limited to the Gulf of Tonkin, a likely inference in light of the geographic focus of that convention. Second, it argues that Chinese artifacts do not constitute a basis for sovereignty. The Vietnamese political counselor in Beijing, for example, argues that Chinese artifacts in Japan do not mean that China owns Japan. Third, Hanoi claims that China never actually exercised sovereignty by occupying the islands in the wake of its 1909 claim, whereas Vietnam is the legal successor to French Indochina, which did claim and occupy the islands in 1933.

In fact, however, the French abandoned the isles in the face of Japanese advances in World War II, during which Japan seized the

Paracels. In 1946 China reclaimed the islands but did not occupy them until 1956, and even then, they only occupied the Amphitrite Group. At the time, the government of the Democratic Republic of Vietnam recognized the Chinese position. Premier Pham Van Dong reportedly stated that "from the historical point of view, these islands are Chinese territory," and in 1958 reiterated that position: "The Government of the Democratic Republic of Vietnam recognizes and supports the Government of the People's Republic of China on its decision concerning China's territorial sea made September 4, 1958."[34]

Hanoi later rejected this position, stating that it was made out of necessity during a time when it depended on China for vital support in its war against the United States. When the government of the Republic of Vietnam (South Vietnam) laid claim to the Paracels and eventually stationed troops in the Crescent Group, Hanoi did nothing to support the Chinese position. In January 1974, after direct U.S. military involvement in South Vietnam had terminated, China seized the Crescent Group from South Vietnamese troops. At the time, with an eye on conquering the South, Hanoi registered its first formal statement expressing dissatisfaction with the Chinese position and called for peaceful resolution of territorial issues. China holds that subsequent Vietnamese objection to its rightful ownership of the Paracels is disingenuous and that Vietnam has no basis for such claims.

China has now strengthened its position in the Paracels to the point where Vietnam has little hope of ever "recovering" them. The PLA has constructed a 2,700-meter runway on Woody Island capable of servicing small numbers of fighter aircraft, and the PLA Navy has been fairly active in the area.[35]

The most significant Chinese action in the Paracels, however, was its 1996 announcement that is was establishing baselines completely around the islands. The most obvious interpretation of this action was that China was claiming the Paracels as a Chinese archipelago, with rights to all resources both within the baseline and reaching outward from it toward an as-yet-unidentified exclusive economic zone. Vietnam immediately protested the action. It stated that "China had deliberately ignored the provisions of the 1982 Convention of the Law of the Sea on the delineation of base lines concerning the archipelagoes belonging to littoral countries and unilaterally delineated the base line of the Paracel Archipelago as if the islands were an archipelagic nation."[36] In fact, the Chinese action was even more egregious, for in subsequent discussions with ASEAN members, China has made the claim that waters within the baseline are "internal waters." This is tantamount to saying all waters within the baselines are "the good earth" and that neither transit nor innocent passage by foreign vessels would be permitted.[37]

In contrast to Vietnam, China refuses to include the Paracels in the Code of Conduct being negotiated between China and the ASEAN states over the South China Sea. China has also opened the islands to tourists and constructed scientific and communications stations on the islands.[38] Vietnam has repeatedly condemned this construction. A typical Vietnamese reaction is as follows:

> The New China News Agency reported that China had built a satellite relay station on Woody Island to "extend China's security network more than 300 km south of Hainan Island" and "to aid China in its assault on crimes related to weapons, drugs, and smuggling in the Eastern Sea." China also installed telephone booths on Spratly Islands. However, the essence of the issue is not the purpose of controlling smuggling but to "expand into the south of the Eastern Sea, step by step conquering the islands in the region. . . ." The Vietnamese Foreign Ministry pointed out: "Vietnam's stance regarding the Spratly and Paracel Archipelagoes is clear. Vietnam is fully justified to assert its sovereignty over the two archipelagoes. With regard to the issues under dispute, Vietnam advocates striving for a fundamental and lasting solution through peaceful negotiations. While promoting talks it is necessary to maintain stability on the basis of the status quo, and the parties concerned should exert self-restraint and refrain from any action that may further complicate the situation. We consider any illegal action by foreign countries concerning the two archipelagoes a violation of Vietnam's territorial sovereignty and invalid. We deem that the above-cited plan is not conducive to the relations between the two countries and the settlement of disputes in the Eastern Sea."[39]

Vietnamese government officials continue to assert their country's sovereignty over the Paracels. Government spokespersons typically react to any action that denies Vietnam's claim to the islands. For example, when China announced a temporary ban on fishing in the South China

Sea in 1999, the Vietnamese foreign ministry responded by reasserting Vietnam's sovereignty over the islands.

> Vietnam has time and again affirmed that it has sufficient historical evidences and legal basis to prove its indisputable sovereignty over the Hoang Sa [Paracels] and Truong Sa [Spratly] archipelagoes. . . . Any action by any country on or around Hoang Sa and Truong Sa archipelagoes as well as in Vietnam's exclusive economic zones and continental shelf without the Vietnamese Government's consent is violation of Vietnam's sovereignty and sovereign rights over these zones.[40]

The possibility of petroleum discoveries adds to the dispute. In October 1999 China announced the discovery of natural gas-hydrate, a solid "gas ice" in the seabed of the Paracel Islands. Gas-hydrate is a clean high-power energy source with considerable potential for future development. The discovery is reportedly the first of its kind in China.[41]

In summary, both China and Vietnam have strong claims to the Paracels, but only China has maintained a presence there since 1974. Vietnam has little ability to project power to the Paracels, while China has developed the islands for cultural, economic, and military use. The importance of the Paracels to Vietnam, then, appears less in any real hope of "recovering" them as in using them as a bargaining chip in anticipated negotiations over bilateral disputes in the Spratly Islands. There Vietnam's policy of maintaining the status quo supports its favorable position relative to China, but at the same time that policy undercuts its claims in the Paracels where Vietnam has no presence whatsoever.

The Spratly Islands

The Spratly "islands" consist of some 200 "features," with a combined land area of less than three square kilometers.[42] The vast majority of the features are cays, reefs, and rocks barely protruding the surface of the water. They are, for the most part, uninhabitable. They have, however, become a focal point of considerable contention not only between China and Vietnam, but also among the other claimants: Malaysia, the Philippines, and Taiwan. Both China and Vietnam claim all the Spratly Islands, while the others claim varying portions of them.

The Chinese claim is based primarily on history. Beijing asserts that Chinese ships visited and conducted business with various islets in the Spratlys as early as the Three Kingdom period (A.D. 220–265) and that Chinese fishermen and traders developed the area.[43] Significantly, this Chinese claim is based on periods of expansion, when it controlled its southern neighbors down to the kingdom of Champa, on what is now the central coast of Vietnam. The connotation of this rationale for Vietnam is that the Middle Kingdom is reasserting the dominant role it had over Vietnam for a thousand years. Just as it does with the Paracels, China claims the Spratlys based on the 1887 Sino-French demarcation of the Gulf of Tonkin. Hanoi rejects both of these historical claims, the former because of its status as an independent nation, and the latter because it views the 1887 Convention as applicable only to the Gulf of Tonkin.

China never exercised effective control over the Spratlys before World War II, and in 1928 a Chinese commission actually reported that the southern boundary of Chinese territory extended to and included the Paracel Islands. With the defeat of Japan in World War II, however, China seized the opportunity of asserting a claim when General Douglas MacArthur directed all Japanese north of the 16th parallel to surrender to the Republic of China.[44] In 1947 the Chinese Nationalist Government issued a map on which nine dotted lines circumscribed nearly all the South China Sea. According to cartographic convention, this meant China claimed sovereignty over all the islands enclosed within those dotted lines. However, with the exception of a brief postwar stay at the former Japanese submarine station on Itu Aba, China never occupied any of the Spratly Islands until the 1980s.[45]

Vietnam also claimed the Spratlys based on history. Like Beijing, it put forth claims to the Spratlys based on records of ship visits and artifacts found on some of the features as evidence of a Vietnamese presence. It also argues that it is the rightful successor to France, which had outposts on a few of the islands as part of French Indochina during the 1930s. However, Vietnam's principal claim appears to be its present occupation of numerous features throughout the Spratlys.

From 1946 to 1975 the Democratic Republic of Vietnam, as it was then known, was preoccupied fighting its wars first with France and then with the U.S.-supported regime in South Vietnam. It had little time to focus on the Spratlys. Moreover, it was so dependent on

China for logistical and other forms of support in both wars that it actually recognized Chinese claims to the Spratlys at one point.[46] Hanoi changed this position after it conquered South Vietnam. Sovereignty over the Spratlys had become important after Mobil Oil discovered oil off nearby southern Vietnam in the early 1970s. In 1973 the South Vietnamese forces had occupied five Spratly features. A year later, just after the South Vietnamese government had announced its intention to explore for oil in the western part of the Paracels (which South Vietnamese troops had occupied in 1969), PLA air and naval forces attacked and displaced the Vietnamese garrison there. A few days later South Vietnamese forces occupied several additional features in the Spratlys.[47]

With the end of the Vietnam War, Hanoi continued Saigon's policy of occupation, moving forces onto six features in 1975.[48] China was unable to react to these Vietnamese actions at the time because of its own political and military weakness. It was still absorbed with the Cultural Revolution, and its naval and air forces did not have the capability to project power southward over 800 nautical miles from its nearest bases on Hainan Island. Moreover, Hanoi had a friend in Moscow, and the Soviet Pacific Fleet had found a new home in Cam Ranh Bay. The Soviets not only provided Vietnam a perceived security blanket vis-a-vis China, but also stimulated further Vietnamese hunger for the Spratlys by governmental studies predicting huge reserves of oil and gas under the islands.

Under these conditions, China bristled while Vietnam continued its policy of occupying as many features in the Spratlys as possible. By 1987, however, Beijing had concluded that there were substantial oil and gas resources in the south-central zone of the Spratlys and that Vietnamese occupation of numerous features in that area threatened to preclude any future Chinese access to those resources. Accordingly, Beijing dispatched "scientific" expeditions to the area, together with oceanographic research vessels backed by PLA Navy ships. This activity disturbed Vietnam, which dispatched aircraft and ships to the region to monitor the Chinese activity, which by then included landing personnel on several reefs. In March 1988 Chinese warships approached Vietnamese ships that Beijing claimed were harassing Chinese scientific teams on the reefs. In the ensuing confrontation, the Chinese ships attacked and sank two Vietnamese ships, killing some 70 Vietnamese sailors in the process. China then occupied six reefs and established Fiery Cross as its main naval outpost in the Spratlys.[49] China finally had a physical presence in the Spratlys.

To reinforce its presence in the Spratlys, China occupied two additional features in 1992, forcing Vietnamese forces out of one of them. It has since maintained a naval presence in the Spratlys. In 1992 the Chinese National People's Congress passed a "Law of the People's Republic of China on the Territorial Sea and the Contiguous Zone," in which it claimed all islands in the Spratlys (and most of the rest of the South China Sea) as Chinese territory.[50] As noted above, Beijing followed this bold claim in 1996 with the establishment of coastal baselines that included those circumscribing the Paracel Islands. At the time Beijing declared it "will announce the remaining baselines of the territorial sea of the People's Republic of China at another time."[51] The implications for the Spratlys are quite clear. At some future date, possibly when China has a better ability to project naval and air power, China may opt to circumscribe the Spratlys with baselines, just as it did in the Paracels.

The possibility of such an outcome terrifies the Vietnamese. The fact that the 1988 incident took place as the Soviet military presence in Vietnam was dramatically declining was not lost on Hanoi. Moreover, Hanoi recognizes that its military position in the Spratlys is weakening. Consequently, during the 1990s Vietnam sought to occupy even more outposts on the Spratlys, constructing lighthouses, fishermen's quarters, scientific stations, and other identifiers of a Vietnamese presence. Vietnam currently occupies 32 separate Spratly features.[52] In addition, Hanoi announced in February 2001 that it had decided to establish a local government for the islands with its administrative headquarters in its coastal province of Binh Thuan.[53]

Vietnamese policy toward the Spratlys is threefold. First, it seeks to strengthen its ability to defend its position in the area. Hanoi has established military garrisons on numerous features and has equipped them with small arms and crew-served defensive weapons. It also maintains a close military relationship with Russia, allowing a small Russian presence at Cam Ranh Bay and increasing its acquisitions of Russian armaments. Vietnam, for example, has over a hundred MiG-21s and some 65 Su-22s. Although these older aircraft cannot compete with more modern Chinese fighters, they do have the range to cover the

Spratlys while the Chinese aircraft presently do not. Moreover, Vietnam has purchased a dozen Su-27 fighters and four Tarantul-class missile boats with surface-to-surface missiles that could give Beijing reason to pause in deciding whether to use force in the Spratlys.[54] Although overall Vietnamese air and naval forces pale in comparison to those of its Chinese neighbor, the lack of effective Chinese attack aircraft with the range needed to cover the Spratlys means that Vietnam, for the time being, can provide a modest military deterrent to Chinese use of force in the area.

The second feature of Vietnamese policy is diplomatic and emphasizes maintenance of the status quo and peaceful settlement of disputes. "While positively promoting negotiations for a fundamental and durable solution to the disputes, all countries involved should maintain stability based on the status quo and exercise self restraint, refraining from any action that would make the situation more complicated. . . . Vietnam has always maintained a consistent stance that any dispute over the overlapping areas on the East Sea [Spratly Islands] should be solved through peaceful negotiations on the basis of respect for international law, especially the 1982 United Nations Convention on the Law of the Sea, and the 1992 Manila Declaration on the East Sea."[55] Of course this policy redounds to Vietnam's advantage, because it controls four times the number of features in the Spratlys as China or any of the other claimants do.

Third, Hanoi responds to any incident or action by China or other claimants by immediately reasserting its sovereignty over the islands. For example, during recent years, Hanoi reacted to the following events:

1. When the government on Taiwan issued a map showing Taiwanese administration of the Paracels and Spratlys, the Vietnamese foreign ministry stated that "any claim by outsiders over these two archipelagoes is a violation of Vietnam's territorial integrity and is null and void."[56]
2. In reaction to a Chinese journal reporting that China approved a "general scientific survey and study of Nansha [Spratly] Islands and adjacent areas" that estimated reserves of 90 thousand tons of oil and 8 to 10 billion cubic meters of natural gas, Vietnam asserted its sovereignty over all the Spratlys.[57]
3. When China announced a fishing ban in the Paracels and Sprat-

lys from 1 June to 31 July 1999, the Vietnamese foreign ministry announced that "Vietnam has time and again affirmed that it has sufficient historical evidences and legal basis to prove its indisputable sovereignty over the Hoang Sa (Paracels) and Truong Sa [Spratly] archipelagoes."[58] "Any action taken by another country relating to the Hoang Sa and Truong Sa archipelagoes as well as in Vietnam's exclusive economic zone and continental shelf without the Vietnamese Government's consent is violation of Vietnam's sovereignty and sovereign rights over these zones."[59]

4. When China proposed to the Philippines that the two countries share use of Vanh Khan (Mischief Reef), the foreign ministry expressed its "deep concern" and reiterated Hanoi's claim to the Spratlys, including Mischief Reef.[60]

5. After Manila charged that Vietnamese troops fired on a Philippine Air Force plane in the northern part of the Spratlys, the foreign ministry again asserted Vietnam's sovereignty over the Spratlys.[61]

Both China and Vietnam regard settlement of the sovereignty issue in the Spratlys as something that cannot be resolved at present. The issue is complicated by the relatively unsubstantiated nature of their historical claims, the uncertainty of finding substantial petroleum reserves, and the fact that Malaysia, the Philippines, and Taiwan also have claims. China and Vietnam have thus focused recent efforts on settling territorial disputes in those areas that offered the best hope for resolution—the completed land border agreement and agreement on the delimitation of the Gulf of Tonkin. The Chinese take the position that they will allow joint development in the Spratlys and the rest of their "historic waters" in the South China Sea, but are adamant that all the Spratlys belong to China and always have. Thus the negotiations, both at the ministerial level and the so-called experts talks between China and Vietnam, have not made progress on the issue of sovereignty in the Spratlys.[62]

Given this situation, the attention of both countries has centered on confidence-building measures (CBMs). There is a long history to ASEAN efforts, both at the governmental and unofficial Track II level, to reach agreement on CBMs for the South China Sea. Suffice it to point out in the context of current Sino-Vietnamese competition for the Spratlys, especially in view of their armed confrontations there in 1988 and 1992, that both sides have participated in both bilateral and multilateral discussions of this topic. China and Vietnam, for example, both claim to support the 1992 ASEAN Declaration on the South China Sea that calls for peaceful resolution of disputes. More recently, Vietnam, along with the Philippines, drafted a code of conduct for the behavior of claimant states in the South China Sea. Subsequently adopted by ASEAN, the ASEAN draft was presented by Vietnam and the Philippines to the Chinese in a meeting in Bangkok in March 2000.

China, however, presented its own draft, with several notable differences that affect the Sino-Vietnamese relations. First, the ASEAN draft referred to the "South China Sea" as the referent point of all discussion, whereas the China draft referred specifically to the Spratlys in discussion on the resolution of disputes. By leaving out the Paracels in this manner, China sought to isolate Vietnam from the other ASEAN claimants, none of which has an interest in the Paracels.[63] Second, the Chinese draft calls for joint development to include exploration and exploitation of resources, whereas the ASEAN draft does not. Hanoi, however, realizes that it cannot conduct any resource exploration or exploitation without the consent of China, which means a retreat from its claim of full sovereignty over all the Spratlys. Third, the ASEAN draft calls for the parties "to refrain from action of inhabiting or erecting structures in presently uninhabited islands, reefs, shoals, cays and other features in the Disputed Area."[64]

With so many features already occupied, this restriction affects Vietnam only at the margins, but for China it could lock in its present small number of occupied features in the Spratlys. Notably, the Chinese draft omits any such language, leading to the conclusion that Beijing may be planning further structures in the South China Sea as part of a policy of "creeping assertiveness."[65]

A final point of disagreement between China and Vietnam has to do with the definition of the Spratlys. Beijing claims that the Nansha (Spratly) Islands extend westward toward the coast of southern Vietnam and include the principal offshore area known to the Vietnamese as Tu Chinh in the Con Son Basin. Vietnam, however, rejects this claim as preposterous, and points to this offshore area as clearly within Vietnam's legitimate exclusive economic zone (EEZ).

The Con Son Basin

Of the four areas of contention between China and Vietnam, none appears more galling to the Vietnamese than that of the Con Son Basin. Mobil Oil first discovered significant petroleum reserves off the coast of southern Vietnam in 1974. After its conquest of South Vietnam in 1975, Hanoi entered a joint venture, Vietsovpetrol, with the Soviet Union. The joint effort initially did well, reopening the Mobil field known as White Tiger (Bach Ho). Production exceeded 100,000 barrels a day by the end of the 1980s. Hanoi was enthusiastic. It allocated blocks to foreign oil companies over a wide area out to 200 miles from its southeastern coast and announced plans to expand operations to nearby Blue Dragon and Big Bear fields. Both of these fields, though well within the 200-nautical-mile exclusive economic zone claimed by Vietnam, were dangerously close to an extension of China's infamous nine dotted lines that demarcated its claims in the South China Sea.

China did not wait long to react to the growing Vietnamese offshore effort. In May 1992 the China National Offshore Oil Company (CNOOC) signed an agreement with the Crestone Energy Corporation, a small Denver-based firm, to explore the 25,000 square kilometers of ocean floor known as Wan-an Bei 21 (Vanguard Bank), just to the east of Vietnam's Big Bear and Blue Dragon fields. Vietnam immediately protested the move. The Crestone concession was 600 miles from Hainan Island, the nearest undisputed Chinese territory, but China vowed to dispatch naval vessels to protect the U.S. crews as necessary.[66] The Chinese reference to the U.S. crews rankled the Vietnamese, who had previously allowed Mobil Oil Company back into the area just west of Wan-an Bei. When Chinese rigs eventually entered the area with U.S. firms working in zones claimed by both countries, the situation grew tense. In 1995 Vietnam drove off a Chinese seismic survey ship in the Crestone block, after which Chinese warships blockaded a Vietnamese oil-drilling rig in the Mobil area.[67]

Sino-Vietnamese differences in the Con Son Basin are not likely to be resolved any time soon. Both sides view the area as having considerably more reserves than outside observers believe possible. A Chinese report estimates the reserves of the sea area of the Wan-an Bei (WAB) at 17.6 billion tons of oil.[68] Vietnam, meanwhile, claims reserves of 1.7 billion barrels. It points to existing oil production of 290,000 barrels a day, and claims an expected increase to 540,000 barrels a day by 2005.[69] In addition, Vietnam plans to exploit gas reserves it estimates at 100 billion cubic meters and plans major gas exploration and pipelines in the coming years.[70] Vietnam plans to use the gas to fuel electric, petrochemical, and fertilizer plants and to refine its crude oil at a new plant to be constructed at Dung Quat in a poor area of central Vietnam. Petroleum already accounts for 13 percent of Vietnam's exports.[71]

Given the importance of offshore oil and gas to its overall economy, Hanoi naturally has reacted strongly to Chinese activity off its coast. It has repeatedly condemned the Chinese claims. As with the Spratlys, these condemnations occur in reaction to Chinese activities that imply sovereignty over the area. Thus in 1998, when China initiated a "scientific survey" along with Crestone, the foreign ministry declared that the survey clearly violated Vietnam's sovereignty over the Tu Chinh area on Vietnam's continental shelf.

The Tu Chinh area is in Vietnam's exclusive economic zone and continental shelf. The area has no connection to the Truong Sa (Spratly) archipelago. Vietnam has repeatedly declared that Vietnam considers illegal the contract signed between the Chinese Overseas Oil Company and the Crestone company of the United States and demands the contract's annulment. That China cooperates with a U.S. company to prospect for oil in the Tu Chinh area in Vietnam's continental shelf clearly violates Vietnam's sovereignty over its continental shelf and exclusive economic zone.[72]

Vietnam strongly feels international law is on its side. It points to Article 76 (1) of the United Nations Convention on the Law of the Sea that states every state has exclusive rights to a continental shelf to a minimum of 200 nautical miles and that a natural prolongation of the shelf could extend that range to 350 nautical miles. Hanoi further argues that the Chinese claim of ownership of adjacent islands (China occupies seven features in the Spratlys) does not give China, even if it had a legitimate claim in the Spratlys, any rights to Vietnam's continental shelf. Citing the proportionality argument of the law of the sea, Hanoi argues that small islands located far from the mainland of China cannot be established as base points for an EEZ.[73]

Beijing argues that the entire South China Sea, up to and including the WAB (Tu Chinh) and other points within its dotted claim line, constitutes historic Chinese waters and that Beijing has an indisputable right to the resources therein. Beijing also claims that its sovereignty over the nearby Spratlys gives it rights in the area. Hanoi, as pointed out earlier, rejects the "historic waters" argument. It also states that the Spratly claim is unjustified, as Vietnam claims the entire Spratlys, occupies the islands closest to the Tu Chinh, and has an overwhelmingly better claim based on its continental shelf.[74]

If international law appears to favor Vietnam, the balance of military power clearly rests with China. It is true that in the immediate area of the dispute Vietnam could more easily bring its air and naval power to bear. Vietnam has acquired from Russia a dozen Su-27 interceptors and four Tarantul I-class corvettes armed with the P20 Styx surface-to-surface missile and is reportedly constructing with Russian assistance a class of large Uran missile boats.[75] Chinese aircraft do not have the range from Chinese airfields to reach the Con Son Basin.[76] However, China's dominant naval forces, coupled with its overwhelming army advantage along the Sino-Vietnamese border, places enormous risk on any Vietnamese attempt to assert its claims by force. Moreover, the increasing modernization of the PLA and of its air and naval forces places Vietnamese diplomats at a disadvantage, since the political signal is that China will dominate the future of the region and there is no alternative but to accommodate its desires.

The seemingly intractable stalemate over oil and gas exploration in contested areas of the Con Son Basin (that is, in areas east of China's claim line) may have a solution in joint development. Although not desirable from Vietnam's viewpoint, it would at least offer a share in and production within the 60-nautical-mile portion of the continental shelf claimed by China. The solution would accord well with China's oft-repeated statement that it will postpone the sovereignty question in favor of joint development.

Bringing additional pressure on Vietnam in this regard is the recent proposal to Beijing by the Russian External Economic Federation, Zarubeznheft, that it plans to enter into joint exploitation for oil in Vietnam's Dai Hung field and in the Gulf of Tonkin.[77] Dai Hung is just outside the Chinese claim line, but it is close enough to prevent full exploitation by Vietnam. As a result, neither Vietnam nor China has exploited it or other contested blocks. The fact that Vietnam's old patron, Russia, is making such a proposal may make joint development a last recourse for Vietnam. It may compel Vietnam, as in centuries past, to yield its oft-repeated position in deference to its strong northern neighbor.

Summary

Of all the areas of Sino-Vietnamese contention, the South China Sea appears to be both the most intractable and the most dangerous. Although the current effort by both nations to build a better relationship continues, the fact that the South China Sea involves issues of national sovereignty, economic well-being, and political prestige portends a difficult road ahead. The agreement on demarcation of the Gulf of Tonkin, while reducing the likelihood of local conflict in that area, reflects Chinese intransigence in pursuing its claims in the Sea, as well as Vietnamese accommodation to growing Chinese assertiveness. The solution to the Gulf thus argues poorly for an equitable settlement of the more difficult problems in the Spratlys and the Con Son Basin. The Paracels appear to be nothing more than a Vietnamese bargaining chip in negotiations over these two areas.

While both Chinese and Vietnamese claims to the Spratlys appear weak, Vietnam's claim to the Con Son Basin appears particularly strong. Moreover, the basin holds far better prospects for commercial petroleum exploitation, because it is, in contrast to the Spratlys, in shallow waters on the continental shelf. Its proximity to Vietnam and long distance from China renders it a likely candidate for international appeals by Hanoi for support of its position. Yet the very prospect of discovering additional petroleum reserves increases its perceived value to energy-deficient China. Of all the areas of the South China Sea, therefore, the one with the most potential for Sino-Vietnamese conflict is the Con Son Basin.

For the immediate future, China appears content to maintain its claim to sovereignty over all territory in the South China Sea while intimating that joint development of ocean resources may be possible in the future. Vietnam's concerns are that the implications of this view are detrimental to its own claims in the short term and that the consequences of a gradually increasing Chinese maritime presence in the region put those claims at risk in the long term.

These concerns impel Vietnam to negotiate a "solution" as early as possible, while joining with its ASEAN neighbors in pursuing confidence-building measures that it hopes will constrain the use of force by China. Vietnam's problem is that China takes a much longer view of the situation and is prepared to wait for a more propitious time to pursue its claims more assertively. Consequently, Sino-Vietnamese disputes in the South China Sea are likely to remain at best an irritant in bilateral relations for the foreseeable future.

CHAPTER 5

Sino-Vietnamese Economic Relations

Despite a slowdown in economic performance during the last two years of the 1990s, the leaders of Vietnam greeted the twenty-first century with considerable rhetorical optimism. Calling on the population to accelerate production and fulfill socioeconomic targets for the coming years, President Tran Duc Luong described Vietnam as embarking on "the path of industrialization and modernization under the direction of socialism for the goal of a prosperous population, a powerful nation, and an equitable and civilized society."[1]

These and other statements by Vietnamese leaders reflect an expectation of modernization with some basis in recent Vietnamese economic performance. During the first seven years of the 1990s, Vietnam managed an average annual gross domestic product (GDP) growth rate of 8.4 percent. Its poverty reduction program appeared successful, with the number of people below the poverty line dropping from 58 to 37 percent between 1992–93 and 1997–98, and the number below the food poverty line dropping from 25 to 15 percent.[2] During the same period, Vietnam attracted foreign direct investment (FDI) at an average rate of $4.4 billion per year.[3] Export growth averaged nearly 10 percent annually and inflation was under control. Vietnamese leaders felt their country had reached the "takeoff stage" in economic development.[4]

That expectation, however, is rife with overoptimism. First, the relatively high growth rates of the 1990s were from the low basis of an economy devastated by war and ill-conceived economic policies. The per capita income of Vietnam in 1990 was a paltry $210, far below that of its neighboring Association of Southeast Asian Nations (ASEAN) countries.[5] Second, the growth that did take place was to a significant degree based on inflated land values, cheap labor, and the stimulus of foreign donors that made Vietnam one of the largest recipients of foreign assistance in the world. Although Vietnam did make structural changes to accelerate production in the agricultural sector, and petroleum production accelerated, the overall economy remained sluggish. The problem manifested itself clearly in the late 1990s, as the growth rate slowed to an average 3.8 percent in 1998 and 1999. International confidence in the Vietnamese economy also eroded, as FDI dropped to less than a third of the average annual pace of the 1991–97 period.[6]

Hanoi pointed to the Asian economic crisis of the late 1990s as the principal cause of its relative economic slowdown. Vietnamese leaders continued to express optimism that a turnaround in the economies of Asia, coupled with large external developmental assistance, would help revitalize its admittedly struggling economy.[7]

The major cause for continued optimism, however, appeared to be a confidence that the development of Vietnam would follow what was perceived as a very successful developmental path blazed by China. Vietnamese leaders looked across their border at a culture and political system that was closely related to their own, but that had achieved remarkable growth and the beginnings of prosperity within a generation. After all, China had led the world in economic growth for two decades. Its per capita output had doubled every 10 years, and its remarkable productivity growth and high savings rates seemed to prognosticate continued strong performance well into the twenty-first century.[8] Like China, Vietnam had a traditional agrarian economy, had emerged during the twentieth century from the shadow of colonialism, had established a socialist economic system, and had an industrious labor force. Moreover, Vietnam saw China's development hinge overwhelmingly on its coastal region, which Vietnam shared in abundance. Vietnam, however, lacked the economic drag of China's huge but less productive interior regions.

Moving toward a Chinese Model

The Socialist Republic of Vietnam had not always looked to China as an economic model. In 1975, after their victorious unification of the country, Vietnamese leaders strove to modernize by exhorting their population to apply the same energy to attain economic independence in the 1975–80 five-year plan as they had in the struggle for political independence a few years earlier.[9] With China in the midst of the Cultural Revolution, emulating China was the last thing Hanoi wanted to do. Hanoi saw a Chinese economy in chaos and was not inclined to emulate it, regardless of the state of political relations between the two countries. Yet relations between China and Vietnam in the late 1970s and the 1980s were anything but cordial. The breakdown of relations that led to the border war of 1979 had led Vietnamese leaders to castigate the Chinese as "the great Han expansionists." The continuation of sporadic hostility along the border until well into the late 1980s reinforced an anti-Chinese bias that persisted despite the reversal of Chinese economic fortunes in the 1980s.

Thus, as China began to embrace limited economic reforms under Deng Xiaoping, Vietnam reacted with disdain for the path chosen by China. Its leaders viewed Chinese reforms as a deviation from the true path of socialism and repeatedly urged the population to greater efforts, urging them, in the words of Ho Chi Minh, to move directly from a "primitive agricultural society into a modern socialist one, bypassing the phase of capitalism."[10]

By the early 1980s, it was apparent that the Vietnamese plan was not working. Poverty and malnutrition were endemic and a change in direction was clearly needed. Still, the government clung to its failed economic policies. In so doing it did not look to China. China had abandoned the commune system and had implemented its Agricultural Responsibility System. This system allowed individual farmers and cooperatives to retain and sell for profit a large portion of above-quota rice production and to initiate private plots along the lines of the short-lived Lieberman reforms of the Soviet Union in the mid-1960s. The results for China were outstanding, with agricultural production soaring in a matter of just a few years. In response to a suggestion that Vietnam should allow its farmers incentives similar to those being implemented in China, a Vietnamese official responded by calling Vietnamese farmers "just ignorant peasants," saying, "they don't know anything."[11]

By the time of the sixth party congress in 1986, however, Hanoi had decided to take action. Vietnam's economy had reached crisis proportions. Unemployment was well over 20 percent, inflation in triple digits, malnutrition widespread, poverty ubiquitous, starvation not unknown, and the population apathetic. Soldiers returning from Cambodia seeking employment added to the trauma, and antigovernment rumblings were beginning to be heard. To address this crisis, the leadership announced at this party congress a platform of economic reform that became known as *doi moi*. Typically translated as "renovation," *doi moi* began implementation in a significant way in 1989, with significant opening of the country to international trade, limited private enterprises, and foreign investment.

The most important change in Vietnam, however, occurred in the most important sector of the economy, agriculture, and was patterned after China's agricultural reform system. The focus of the reform was the transformation of inefficient and bureaucratic agricultural cooperatives and collectives to family-based farms with incentives for increased production. The system was patterned after that of China in three respects. First, farmers were allowed to grow certain crops on private plots around their houses for family needs or for barter or sale. Second, the cultivation of fish on agricultural land was encouraged, so that Vietnam's numerous ponds became important sources of protein. Third, farmers were allowed initially to market rice produced above quota, and later all rice, at prevailing prices. Known as *vuon ao truong*, the new incentives gave Vietnamese farmers unprecedented economic freedom and resulted in a dramatic turnaround of the agricultural sector.[12] Within a decade, Vietnam moved from near-starvation in many areas to agricultural self-sufficiency, with annual rice export volume of over 3 million metric tons.

Following the Chinese way of economic development was not, however, a foregone conclusion in the early 1990s. During those years, Vietnam was actively seeking economic models, not to imitate, but to adapt to Vietnam's particular circumstances. Because of its success in modernization, China was one possible model, but economic advisers in the prime minister's office looked to Singapore and Taiwan as more appropriate alternatives. Both presented a combination of strong central political direction and domestic stability. Both had a sustained record of high economic growth. Vietnamese saw the Taiwan model as having the additional advantage of having demonstrated a successful land reform program decades earlier.[13] Moreover, both Singapore and

Taiwan led the foreign investment that was beginning to stimulate certain sectors of the Vietnamese economy. Both countries excelled in and led their investment in Vietnam with small-scale business enterprises.

It is interesting to note that by the mid-1990s the three states that Vietnam looked to as models of economic development all had Chinese populations. Nevertheless, as the 1990s progressed, Vietnam increasingly looked to the People's Republic of China as its principal model of development.[14] By the end of the decade, Vietnamese leaders who had previously castigated China as the enemy of Vietnam were flocking to Beijing to pay their respects and to solicit Chinese advice for Vietnam's emerging economy. Although largely for economic purposes, their travels to China began to take on the appearance of pilgrimages by a tributary state.

The Pilgrimages

Traditional Vietnamese subservience to China appeared to be well entrenched by the end of the 1990s. Delegation after delegation of Vietnamese government, party, and economic and cultural groups beat a path to Beijing to sing the praises of Vietnam's mighty neighbor. Back in Hanoi, Vietnamese leaders at the highest levels repeated this praise. The tone of Vietnam's approach to China is well illustrated by the following statements of top Vietnamese officials in 1999 alone.

In February General Secretary Le Kha Phieu visited Beijing. On the first day of his visit he proclaimed: "Since its establishment, and especially during 20 years of reform and open-door policies, China has obtained great achievements. I would like to seize the opportunity of my trip to study China's precious experiences in building socialism with Chinese identity."[15] The next day, accompanied by Minister of Economic Affairs Phan On, Phieu said he saw "good momentum of rapid economic development in a rural village of Chengdu City's suburbs, the Zhuhai Special Economic Zone, and the Guangzhou Economic Development Zone in Guangdong. This proves that a correct line can make the country and people prosperous."[16] Phieu qualified his remarks somewhat by adding that while China will continue to "firmly take the road of socialist reform and opening up that conforms to China's characteristics," Vietnam will "firmly take the road of socialist reform that conforms to Vietnam's characteristics."[17] The general secretary said he highly valued the achievements of China both in restructuring its economy and in opening its doors to external trade and cooperation.[18] Coming from the highest levels of Vietnam's power structure, the Phieu statements clearly portray Vietnam paying at least lip service to China's leading role in socialist economic development.

This theme was reiterated during the visits of two Vietnamese deputy prime ministers. In May 1999 Nguyen Tan Dung was quoted as flatly stating that Vietnam "aims at learning from China's advanced experiences in facilitating reform and opening up, and in developing socialist undertakings with Chinese characteristics," especially "the advanced experience of China's social and economic progress."[19] In July Nguyen Cong Tan was quoted as saying, "The great achievements made by China in economic construction are yielding very important effect on the stability and development in this region and even in the world. . . . China's policy of reform and opening up has enabled China to make the great achievements in economic construction. Particularly in 1998, China successfully resisted the impact of the unprecedented, serious natural calamities at home, and maintained sustained economic development."[20]

In September 1999, on the occasion of the 50th anniversary of the PRC, Prime Minister Phan Van Khai was even more eloquent in his praise, stating, "the Chinese people are right to place their full confidence in the Communist Party of China. . . . The achievements of the Chinese people over the past 50 years have proved the wisdom of the Chinese people's choice."[21] Khai was quoted as saying that the facts show that China followed the right way, and offered a wise choice for other people in the world.[22] The following month Politburo member Pham The Duyet visited Beijing. In his meeting with National People's Congress Chairman Li Peng, Duyet spoke highly of China's experiences in socio-economic development and maintaining Communist Party leadership.[23]

More recently, Vietnamese leaders have extended their praises of China in the military field. For example, during the February 2001 visit of Chinese defense minister Chi Haotian to Hanoi, Vietnamese defense minister Pham Van Tra was quoted as promising that Vietnam would implement the "mutual understanding" reached between the two countries in the border areas and would strive to "further develop cooperation between the two countries in the military field."[24] Both Defense Minister Tra and Vietnamese Communist Party general secretary Le Kha Phieu were quoted as telling Minister Chi that Vietnam appreciates "the great achievements gained in China's reform and opening-up."[25] Apparently, the recognition of China's great achievements in "opening up" stimulated emulation by the Vietnamese leaders, in sharp contrast to Ho Chi Minh's recognition that the strength of Vietnam's modernization lies not in dependency on a neighboring Asian country, but on the source of that modernization, which was the West.[26]

Chinese "Patrimony"

Why, one might ask, does Vietnam indulge in such praise? Undoubtedly there is an element of flattery involved, but the words of Vietnam's leaders also reflect a belief that the future of their country depends on both emulating the Chinese system and benefiting from Chinese economic assistance. They perceive China as having the most dynamic economic system in Asia, and for that reason it is becoming a great power on which Vietnam will have to depend for much-needed developmental assistance. In this view, China holds the key to Vietnam's future. That future will see China as the most powerful nation in Asia, and a big brother (a patron) on whom Vietnam can rely in its quest for prosperity.

Prime Minister Phan Van Khai succinctly reflects this Vietnamese attitude in his statements. In December 1998 Chinese vice president Hu Jintao visited Hanoi and met with Khai. Khai praised Chinese achievements and thanked the Chinese government and people for their support for Vietnam. He was quoted as stating that he was pleased China has "further boosted its national power and enhanced its position in the world."[27] Two months later Phieu made his aforementioned visit to China. There Phieu met with Li Lanqing, Politburo Standing Committee member and premier of the State Council, and was reported to have thanked Li for China's long assistance to Vietnam.[28]

The Chinese attitude, in contrast, is one of munificence by a greater power to a lesser one. In remarks designed to reinforce the legitimacy of party rule in both countries, Chinese vice president Hu Jintao, a member of the powerful Politburo Standing Committee, told his party counterpart, Pham The Duyet, that Vietnam, under the leadership of the Vietnamese Communist Party (VCP), had made remarkable progress in reform and "opening up" over the past 10 years. He praised VCP enactment of measures to ensure social stability and economic development, gratuitously stating that he was convinced Vietnam would overcome its "temporary difficulties" and realize the goals of industrialization and modernization of its eighth party congress. Duyet lauded "China's achievements over the past more than 20 years, especially the great efforts made by the Chinese party, government, and people in overcoming difficulties caused by the regional economic crisis. . . ."[29]

The Chinese assistance to which Duyet referred included both individual Chinese projects and assistance during the Asian financial crisis of 1997–99. The former focused on highly visible projects designed to have high impact on Sino-Vietnamese relations. A typical example is the Chinese construction of a bridge across the Nam Thi River at Lao Cai. The bridge, constructed in 1999, connects Vietnam and China and has the potential to stimulate additional border trade. Despite this high impact, Vietnamese sources reported that China expended only $1.8 million on its construction.[30]

China's principal assistance during the Asian financial crisis, however, was its decision not to devalue its currency, the renminbi. Although many factors shaped this decision, Chinese leaders emphasized its benefits to neighboring countries. The Chinese foreign ministry, for example, stated that President Jiang Zemin's decision not to devalue the renminbi "truly reflect the country's commitment to helping its ASEAN neighbors during the financial turmoil."[31] The Chinese press further pointed out that this policy was executed despite floods and other natural calamities, a fact that Vietnamese leaders acknowledged in their discussions in Beijing.[32] General Secretary Le Kha Phieu "highly praised the great achievements" of Chinese socialism and thanked China for its help to Vietnam in overcoming the regional financial crisis of the late 1990s.[33] China further pledged to do its share to contribute to regional prosperity through its own development.[34]

Like a new patron, China also gave evidence that it wanted Vietnam to view it as its primary benefactor, to which Vietnam should be duly thankful. During the height of the financial crisis, China's official China News Agency (Xinhua) reported that Vietnam was in serious trouble and that alternative benefactors paled in comparison to China.

> The crisis has inflicted major damage on the Vietnamese economy, with declining exports, reduced foreign investment, and a slowdown in the rate of economic development. Forecasts are that this year's

growth will only be about 3 percent, a sharp drop from the 9 percent of the last two years. The economic depression has led to a big jump in unemployment, and has created problems in the areas of social security and political stability. . . . Vietnam's President Tran Duc Luong visited Russia, while Deputy Prime Minister Nguyen Manh Cam visited the United States. The hope was to expand economic and trade cooperation with the United States and Russia, but the results were insignificant.[35]

Chinese leaders also held out the hope that Chinese trade and investment would soon help pull Vietnam out of its recent lackadaisical economic performance. From 25 February to 2 March 1999, Le Kha Phieu again visited China. During the visit, the two sides signed a "Sino-Vietnamese Agreement on Economic Cooperation" in which they pledged to "give full play to the role of large corporations" and "to cooperate with each other in large projects" as part of an overall effort to expand trade, investment, and technology exchange.[36] State Council president Li Lanqing told Phieu, "there is a need to give further play to the main channeling role of large companies, to expand bulk commodity trade . . . to encourage and support both countries' large cooperative projects, to promote healthy and orderly development of the two countries' border trade, and to strive to raise economic and trade cooperative relations to a new level."[37]

A Reality Check

Closer examination of actual Chinese economic relations with Vietnam, however, reveals a sharply different picture than the verbal exchanges between the two countries' national leaders would indicate. This picture is seen most clearly in the pattern of three areas of foreign exchange with Vietnam: investment, aid, and trade.

According to the government of Vietnam, FDI is critical to the overall modernization of the nation. As part of its policy of "opening up" to the outside world, Vietnam began in 1988 to attract increasing amounts of FDI, and by the mid-1990s, it accounted for over an average 9 percent of GDP.[38]

After over 10 years of experience, however, a pattern has emerged revealing that China is an insignificant factor in this overall effort. To begin with, China is not even listed among the major investment countries of origin. In terms of actual disbursements, Taiwan leads in investment, with cumulative disbursements of $1.4 billion through 1998. Japan is second with $1.2 billion, followed by Singapore and South Korea. In terms of commitments, Singapore is the leading investor, with $5.8 billion, followed by Taiwan, with $4.0 billion; Japan, with $3.3 billion; and South Korea, with $2.9 billion. At $120 million, China ranks 21st among countries investing in Vietnam.[39] Thus the record shows that Chinese investment, compared to that of other nations in Asia and the world, is a pittance. Indeed, the record shows that the Asian nations other than China account for two-thirds of all investment in Vietnam compared to just 1 percent by China. Indeed, during the first seven years since the two countries normalized relations, China had invested a mere $120 million in Vietnam.[40]

There is, moreover, an apparent disagreement between China and Vietnam about the type of investment needed by Vietnam. While Chinese officials repeatedly stress large-scale projects in their meetings with Vietnamese representatives, Vietnam apparently has a different view of the type of economic growth needed. Just a few months after General Secretary Le Kha Phieu gratuitously agreed with his Chinese interlocutors on the need for "large corporations" and "large projects," Vietnamese deputy prime minister Nguyen Cong Tan told Chinese deputy minister of state planning Liu Jiang that Vietnam wished to strengthen further the introduction of small and medium-sized companies.[41] In fact, Minister Tan's reported remarks may reflect a reevaluation of Vietnamese needs inside the government, as Vietnamese high-cost capital intensive industries have demonstrated little in the way of comparative advantage.[42]

The second area of economic exchange, developmental assistance, shows a similar pattern. Chinese assistance to Vietnam has been sparse, with interest-free loans of only $14 million since 1992.[43] China is not even listed among the donor nations that provide virtually all of Vietnam's considerable aid. Most of the "large-scale" aid promised in 1999 was limited to rehabilitation to a few 1950s-era factories built originally with Chinese assistance. In 1998 and 1999, Official Development Assistance (ODA) disbursements averaged 4.5 percent of GDP, while pledges averaged 7.7 percent. The top donor nation by far was Japan, with $369 million disbursed in 1998. Japan was followed by the World

Bank, the Asian Development Bank, and France in that order.[44] In December 1998 Japan pledged over a billion dollars in developmental assistance to Vietnam, and indicated it would add to that figure with additional aid from the Miyazawa Plan for Southeast Asia.[45] Japan provides more assistance to Vietnam in one year than China has provided for the past 25 years.

The third area of economic exchange follows a similar pattern. Trade between the Socialist Republic of Vietnam and the People's Republic of China was halted during the 1979 border war, but resumed in earnest upon normalization of relations in 1991. In that year, bilateral trade totaled a mere $32 million.[46] Eight years later, in 1999, bilateral trade stood at $1.25 billion, a dramatic increase in a relatively short time. The increase should not be overstated, however, not only because it showed no increase from 1998, but also because as a percentage of either country's total trade, particularly that of China's, the amounts are minuscule. China had a total trade of $324 billion in 1998, of which Vietnam accounted for 0.34 percent. Vietnam had a total trade of $20.817 billion, of which China accounted for $1.245 billion, or 6 percent.[47] This relatively small volume of trade is far from what might be expected from neighbors with a 797-mile land border and proximate connecting sea-lanes. The Vietnamese prime minister repeatedly stressed this fact in early 1999, and again in his meeting with Chinese prime minister Zhu Rongji in China in October 1999.[48] Both leaders stated their views that they would attempt to raise the figure to $2 billion in the year 2000 (subsequently accomplished).

From the Vietnamese point of view, there are four additional problems of bilateral trade with China. First is the imbalance in favor of China by a margin of 4.7 to 1. It is running an overall foreign exchange deficit while it reports that China sports a massive surplus, so its deficit with China exacerbates its balance of payments problem.[49] In August 1999 Vietnamese deputy trade minister Nguyen Xuan Quang pointed this out clearly, stating that there is "a serious imbalance in the two countries' trade relations, with Vietnam suffering an increasing trade deficit."[50]

A second problem is that the nature of the trade adversely affects several Vietnamese industries. Hanoi is inundated with Chinese products, such as electrical appliances, hi-fi equipment, air conditioners, toys, and food. Chinese garments, autos, and chemicals are seen to stifle nascent Vietnamese industries. Indeed, Vietnam has raised the infant industries argument with China in an attempt to resuscitate some of its labor-intensive small industries.[51] Moreover, some Vietnamese exports, such as textiles, shoes, audio and video equipment, and handicrafts compete directly with the far larger scale Chinese industries. For example, the village of Bat Trang along the Red River east of Hanoi specializes in ceramics and hopes to increase its export market, but its products compete with the more sophisticated and mass-produced ceramics of China.[52]

The third problem for Vietnam, and one shared by China, is unofficial trade, especially smuggling. Estimated at $500 million in 1998, this trade has flourished along the border and coastal regions in recent years. Both sides appear to be involved. Vietnam claims that Chinese motor bikes, sugar, eggs, and other commodities are routinely smuggled into Vietnam, and that smuggled drugs, including hashish, are exacerbating Vietnam's growing drug problem.[53] China claims that Vietnamese traffickers are illegally smuggling autos and tobacco into southern China. Both governments claim to be working to resolve the problem. In March 1999 their prime ministers pledged to promote "a sound and orderly development of border trade."[54] In July 1999 Vietnamese deputy prime minister Dung called for a review of implementation of antismuggling Government Directive No 853/1997.[55] Two months later Vietnam declared new currency controls at the border.[56]

A major area of concern is the smuggling of petroleum into China from coastal areas near the border. Chinese reports indicate that a large share of the oil consumed in southern China is smuggled into the country by sea, with significant amounts coming from Vietnam. In 1999, for example, China's Customs Department deployed antismuggling vessels to intercept a Vietnamese vessel reportedly smuggling diesel fuel into Nanning. When the Vietnamese vessel tried to escape, the customs vessels fired on it and it burst into flames.[57]

The action reflects a tough line Beijing has taken against smuggling beginning in 1998. Launching a nationwide campaign against smuggling, Beijing appointed Wu Yi, known as the Chinese "Iron Lady," to direct the campaign as head of the State Council's antismuggling effort in the Tonkin Gulf. Wu said that huge amounts of oil are entering southern China via the gulf. Recognizing that corrupt Chinese officials were part of the problem, she directed Chinese Customs to "keep an eye on their own men and guard the doors of the nation."[58]

The Tonkin Gulf (Beibu Wan) presents a difficult problem for other commodities as well. In October 1998 Chinese prime minister Zhu Rongji visited Guangzhou "to listen to countersmuggling reports, including Beibu Wan Action in Guangxi's Beibu Wan.[59] Wu Yi charged that Vietnam has automobile and tobacco bonded warehouses in Mon Cay, on the south side of the Beilun border river, and that these warehouses are "targeted at China." She added the Beilun's "numerous bays and river forks pose great difficulties to the antismuggling forces. Moreover, many of the local inhabitants have made it rich through smuggling, and many customs officials have been bribed." She promised that China would deliver a "telling blow" against the smugglers in the Tonkin Gulf and the Beilun River area.[60]

Smuggling in the gulf continues to be a major source of Sino-Vietnamese friction despite the efforts of people like Wu Yi, with local officials and business persons profiting at the expense of the central governments that lose tax revenue and control of local economies. The Chinese government has admitted that the smuggling deprives it of substantial tax revenues and creates independent centers of wealth. However, local officials and members of the People's Liberation Army are reportedly profiting from the schemes, helping them to exert power and influence along the border regions outside of central government control.

The final problem for Vietnam is that poverty has driven some Vietnamese into not just national deference with respect to China, but also personal subservience. Reported police figures indicate, for example, that 22,000 Vietnamese women and children have been lured to work in Chinese brothels over the past seven years.[61]

The Chinese Model: Perception and Performance

The final and perhaps most important aspect of Vietnam's selecting China as an economic model is the perception that Chinese economic growth has been so outstanding that it is worthy of emulation not only by Vietnam but also by other developing countries worldwide.

Vietnamese prime minister Phan Van Khai clearly stated this position on the occasion of commemorating the 50th anniversary of the founding of the People's Republic of China. Khai was quoted as telling his hosts:

> The Chinese society has been transformed from a semi-feudal, semi-colonial agrarian base to a miraculous economy, with an annual growth rate two and a half times the world average. The 20 years of reform and opening up are particularly remarkable during which China doubled its gross domestic product every 10 years, which would have taken 58 years in Britain, 47 years in the United States, and 34 years in Japan.[62]

Khai went on to say that these facts proved that the Chinese people have followed a right way of development and enabled China to assume an important role both in Asia and in the rest of the world. He said he believed that the practice of the Chinese people has offered a wise choice for other people in the world in their efforts to build a society of fairness, love, prosperity, and happiness.[63]

The facts do not support Khai's apparent enthusiasm. By adopting economic reforms, beginning with the abandonment of communes in favor of limited free enterprise incentives in the agricultural sector, China did attain far more rapid economic growth in the 20 years after 1978 than it did in the preceding 30 years. Nevertheless, the growth was from an exceptionally low base, and like any enterprise in its early growth stage, rapid percentage gains are easier than in its mature stage. Moreover, the oft-repeated 10–12 percent real growth rates registered by China for its overall economy during these years are grossly exaggerated. A World Bank baseline study in 1997 indicated that China's real growth during the 1978 to 1994 period was probably closer to 6.8 percent per year than the higher official figure of 8 percent cited by the Government.[64] Moreover, the rate of decline officially cited is striking, even though Chinese growth is expected to level off in the first years of the twenty-first century.

Alternatives to China as a Model and Economic Partner

In spite of these realities, the official Vietnamese approach to national development remains one of emulation of the Chinese model, in opposi-

Figure 5-1: China's Real Economic Growth Rate: 1994–99

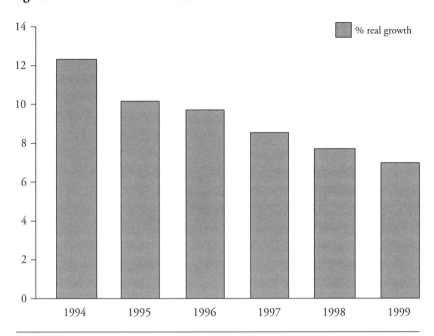

Source: EIU, *Country Report: China* (4th quarter 1999): 6; IMF, *World Economic Outlook*, 1998 and 1999, table 1.1.

tion to alternatives such as the United States, Japan, Taiwan, or other nations of Asia. There are signs, however, that the leadership in Hanoi is beginning to question the wisdom of looking to China as an economic model and principal economic partner. Voices in the office of the prime minister and parts of the trade and foreign ministries have made the case that Russia, Japan, Taiwan, and the United States may have more to offer in the long term.[65]

Looking through the rearview mirror, Hanoi clings to the hope that Russia can some day play a major role in the economic future of Vietnam. At the ASEAN summit conference in Hanoi, Prime Minister Khai said "it is cheaper to do business with Russia, in the experience of Vietnam."[66] In a major policy address, Foreign Minister Nguyen Manh Cam stated that "Vietnam still treasures Russia" and is working to remove its debt problem with it.[67] In 1998, despite foreign debt of $166 billion, Russia still provided Vietnam $110 million in soft loans, one-forth of such overseas loans ($400 million) for that year.[68] The principal Vietnamese economic connection with Russia, however, is oil. In late 1999 the Russian Ministry of Fuel and Energy sent a delegation to Vietnam to reinforce a competitive Russian presence. The delegation lobbied for imports of coal for the Maritime Territory and Kamchatka, and got Vietnam to sign a framework agreement for gas exploration and development in the northern part of the Gulf of Tonkin and off central Vietnam (whose reserves the delegation estimated at 700 billion cubic meters). Further south, the Russian-Vietnamese consortium, Vietsovpetrol, accounts for $430 million in annual exports, of which the Big Bear and White Tiger fields accounted for $230 million.[69]

Japan also is seen as a model in some respects. As indicated earlier, Japan is the leading provider of official developmental assistance to Vietnam. It is also Vietnam's principal trading partner and the third largest investor in Vietnam.[70] The combination of these factors makes Japan the most important nation to Vietnam's overall economic well-being. Vietnam recognizes this role and paid special tribute to Japan for its assistance in helping Vietnam through the Asian financial crisis.[71] Vietnam also pays close attention to visiting Japanese delegations. For example, the state-run television network covered the Keidanren head's visit to Vietnam in detail, stating that the visit showed "the importance Japan places on our economy."[72] Despite paying it great attention, however, Vietnam tends to view Japan as a large-scale, heavily industrialized economic superpower whose relevance to its agrarian and small-scale industries is quite remote.

A more appropriate model for Vietnam, especially in contrast to China, might be Taiwan. Like Vietnam, Taiwan developed from an agrarian base. It also executed a successful land reform program and developed steadily to become a top economic performer in Asia. Taiwan is the third largest investor in Vietnam, with over $4 billion in cumulative commitments. It is also Vietnam's third largest trading partner.[73] With 1,500 businesses investing and 180,000 Taiwan businessmen visiting Vietnam annually, Taiwan has created some 300,000 to 400,000 jobs in that country. The vast majority of these are in small business enterprises that produce foods like cooking oil, instant noodles, and flour and in textiles, footwear, motorcycle manufacturing, and information technology.[74] Taiwan sees Vietnam as having a loose underground economy and a hardworking people. It has executed a three-year agreement to allow Vietnamese workers into Taiwan.[75]

Of all the potential nations upon which Vietnam may pin its economic hopes for the future, however, the United States may be the most significant. Hanoi knows that if it can tap into the U.S. market in a major way, the economic benefits for Vietnam would be immense. Foreign Minister Nguyen Manh Cam, in a major speech on Vietnam's foreign policy to the 10th National Assembly's fourth session, stated that "one opinion" (with which he appeared to agree) is that a great depression would not occur as a result of the Asian financial crisis, because the U.S. and West European economies are so strong. Although two-way trade with the United States is less than a billion dollars annually, the hope of pragmatic Vietnamese leaders is that normal trade relations with the United States will dramatically expand Vietnam's exports, providing an engine of growth that can help spur Vietnam's recovery.

Why, then, did Vietnam delay for one year the signing of the U.S.-Vietnam Bilateral Trade Agreement (BTA) that was reached in Hanoi on 25 July 1999? One explanation is that delays in the United States were responsible. At the time of the agreement, U.S. president Bill Clinton was quoted by Xinhua as saying that he hoped the BTA would be completed "very soon." "I will review the agreement carefully and consult further with the Congress and the government of Vietnam in the hope that we will be able to move on to finalization, formal signature, and the establishment of normal trade relations very soon."[76] Delays in the Congress, resulting from concerns about POW and MIA matters, are considered possible reasons.

More plausible explanations, however, relate to Vietnam. First, Vietnam's relations with China would be affected. One of the explanations that has been given for Vietnam's slowness in confirming the agreement is that Hanoi was concerned about China's reaction.

> In July Vietnam made major policy concessions in its negotiations with the United States on a preliminary draft of a trade agreement. Yet in September the Politburo balked and no agreement was reached. Reports indicated that the small-scale Chinese military incursions into Vietnamese territory might have been responsible for this turnaround. Subsequent reports indicate that Chinese leaders may have been persuading their Vietnamese counterparts to wait until China reached an agreement on trade issues with the U.S. before proceeding.[77]

Another explanation is that the agreement was in jeopardy because of concerns that it would threaten the growing commercial activities of the Vietnamese military. The agreement would, for example, allow U.S. companies to operate on an equal footing in Vietnam with Vietnamese companies. Although it is estimated that the agreement would boost overall commercial activity in Vietnam by $800 million in the first year of operation, it would also allow U.S. companies to compete directly with these commercial enterprises. In 1999 the People's Army of Vietnam (PAVN) operated some 335 commercial enterprises. Some 100,000 soldiers, or 20 percent of all regular military personnel, were engaged in corporate activity in construction, production, and sale of industrial explosives, flight and shipping services, mining, engineering, and garment production. Their annual turnover was estimated at $613 million.[78]

In a similar vein, the BTA may also have threatened Vietnam's state-owned enterprises, which despite their inefficiencies, continue to account for nearly half the gross domestic product.[79]

Conclusions

Despite a significant economic downturn at the end of the 1990s, Vietnamese officials claim to be optimistic that their country will regain the high growth rates that characterized the earlier part of the decade. While some of that confidence results from renewed growth in the region and some from the prospect of increased exports to the United States, much more appears to hinge on the belief that Vietnam will develop and sustain the high growth rates attributed to China. This belief is founded on the idea that Vietnam should pattern the fundamentals of its economic system on that of China. This position reversed an earlier Vietnamese attitude at a time when China was perceived as not only failing economically, but also deviating from socialist ideology. In connection with initiating its own reforms in the late 1980s and early 1990s, Vietnam examined several models of development, but settled ultimately on China.

Vietnamese leaders then began a crescendo of pilgrimages to China, where they extolled the virtues and accomplishments of that country's socialist system. To some extent, their munificent praise may have been flattery to gain China's favor in negotiations on disputed territories, but the weight of evidence points to a belief that Vietnam must adjust to its newly powerful neighbor. China reinforced its superior position in the relationship by stressing its role in helping Vietnam through the Asian financial crisis, by promoting high visibility infrastructure projects, and by denigrating Vietnamese prospects for substantial economic relations with alternative major powers, such as Russia and the United States.

A reality check reveals that Vietnam stands to benefit far more from economic relations with other nations of the region, most notably Japan, South Korea, Taiwan, and several of the ASEAN countries. Compared to these countries, China provides a minuscule amount of direct foreign investment and official developmental assistance, and it is a smaller trading partner. In addition, the potential of the U.S. market exceeds that of China by a wide margin. Moreover, there are significant trade problems between China and Vietnam, including an imbalance in China's favor, the detrimental impact of Chinese exports on infant Vietnamese industries, and an enormous amount of cross-border smuggling. Finally, China has some serious problems in its own development that Vietnamese authorities do not appear to take fully into account as they extol China as an economic model not only for their country, but also for the world. Recent evidence shows that Vietnam's economic reliance on China, together with China's pressure on Vietnam, may have helped delay the conclusion of normal trade relations with the United States.

In light of these factors, it is clear that the leadership in Hanoi pays close attention and respect to Vietnam's economic relations with China for reasons other than national economic benefit. Economics is certainly not the glue that binds these two nations together. In the next chapter, we will examine some of those reasons, including, most important, their shared objective of regime maintenance. For the present we simply conclude that while Vietnam may learn something from China, following the Chinese model is not the way to economic success for Vietnam. Alternative models are needed. The successful free enterprise systems of East Asia, from which Vietnam already derives beneficial trade, aid, and investment, may offer the best path for the future Vietnam.

CHAPTER 6

The Politics of Sino-Vietnamese Relations

As Vietnam accommodates to the perceived rising power of China, the tragic cycle of a historical relationship in which Vietnam paid tribute and requested investiture of its kings threatens to repeat itself. After defeating all its enemies, including China in the border war of 1979, and successfully uniting the country, Vietnam today is once again bowing to the will of China on important internal and external issues. Internally, Hanoi is preoccupied with stability, seeking to achieve it in the same way as China, by maintaining the unchallenged rule of the Communist Party. Externally, while proclaiming diversification, Hanoi tends to take no action inconsistent with Chinese foreign and defense policy.[1]

The attitude of Vietnam is a reflection of a fundamental imbalance in Sino-Vietnamese relations. While Chinese leaders do not consider Vietnam as of great importance to China in any dimension—political, economic, or military—the Vietnamese leadership perceives China as of the utmost importance to Vietnam. Its political influence dominates Hanoi's domestic and foreign policy agenda; its economy provides the principal model for Vietnamese development; and its military power restrains both Vietnam's freedom of action in the South China Sea and its military relations with outside powers. Today there is a growing reliance on Chinese goodwill that overshadows all other Vietnamese international relations—a dependency that threatens to deny Vietnam the very ability to reap the rewards of its own unification and independence.

The Shadow of History

During the lifetime of the current generation of Chinese and Vietnamese leaders, the relationship between their two countries has changed dramatically. The old generation of revolutionary leaders found a fertile training base for their activity in China. It was in Canton (Guangzhou) that Ho Chi Minh organized the Thanh Nien ("coming of age" youth group) that eventually formed the core of the Indochina Communist Party. The Chinese Communist Party also provided a revolutionary model for Ho and assisted his followers in periodically escaping French security. After Mao Zedong seized power, China provided critical supplies and military equipment to turn the tide of battle decisively against the French. China was also among the first to recognize the Democratic Republic of Vietnam. During the "American War," China provided training, logistical support, military equipment, and support troops to the People's Army of Vietnam. More important to Hanoi's ultimate victory, China secured North Vietnam from ground attack by virtue of U.S. fear that such an attack would result in Chinese volunteers entering the war.[2]

Despite this cooperation, described by both sides as being "as close as the lips to the teeth," China and Vietnam found themselves at war in the opening months of 1979. That war is still very fresh in the minds of the leaders of both countries. The principal battles lasted only three weeks. The People's Liberation Army, which had not fought a serious engagement for over 10 years, met Vietnamese military forces that had fought the United States, South Vietnam, and Cambodia— all within the same period. The result was predictable. Organized and trained by the regular forces, Vietnamese militia, supported by regular troops, inflicted heavy losses on the invaders. After several weeks of bitter fighting, culminating with the seizure of major portions of all six of Vietnam's border provinces, including three provincial capitals, the People's Liberation Army (PLA) had lost as many as 75,000 men killed or wounded.[3] It then withdrew back to China, as had innumerable Chinese armies bloodied by Vietnam throughout history.

Although defeated militarily, China did achieve a long-term political goal, which Deng Xiaoping described as "teaching Vietnam a lesson." While Vietnamese troops remained in Cambodia for another 10 years, China had shown Vietnam that it was prepared to use force if Vietnam flouted Chinese interests. The lesson was that China would attack Vietnam if Hanoi erred by pursuing its own interests in disregard of China's position in Asia. In the case at hand, Vietnam had, before the Chinese invasion, invaded Cambodia, whose government China supported. It had aspired for hegemony in Indochina, challenging Beijing's long-term ambitions for a sphere of influence in Southeast Asia. It had persecuted its indigenous Chinese (Hoa) population, driving hundreds of thousands of them across the border into China. It had challenged China's sovereignty in the South China Sea by occupying additional features, and by laying claim to the Paracel Islands that its premier, Pham Van Dong, had previously agreed were Chinese. But most egregious of all, it had consorted and sought alliance with the Soviet Union, then the archenemy of China.

At a deeper level, the 1979 border war revealed core differences in the two sides' perceptions of what they thought the nature of their relationship should be. China felt betrayed. It had provided Ho Chi Minh a "great rear base" from which to organize and gather military strength during his quest for power. It had aided the Viet Minh against the French, culminating in the decisive victory at Dien Bien Phu. It had provided huge quantities of small arms, trucks, and antiaircraft guns, together with over 100,000 Chinese volunteers, to help North Vietnam against the United States.[4]

Beijing felt Hanoi, like a little brother, should be profoundly grateful and follow the Chinese line in important matters. When Vietnam refused and continued its occupation of Cambodia, China pursued a 10-year policy of harassment along the border, including the aforementioned artillery barrages and sporadic raids into Vietnamese territory. In 1988 the PLA Navy sank two Vietnamese vessels in the Spratly Islands. The infamous (from Vietnam's point of view) lesson Deng was teaching was just that—a lesson for the pupil, Vietnam, from the teacher, China. Such was the nature of the relationship expected by China.

Vietnam's perception of the relationship was entirely different. In 1979 it labeled the Chinese "the great Han expansionists," seeking once again to dominate and control its foreign and domestic policy. Having achieved victory over France and the United States in South Vietnam, Hanoi felt it had earned the right to assert independent policies, including preeminence in an Indochina federation in keeping with the last will and testament of Ho Chi Minh. It saw a China in collusion with the United States to subvert its independent stance, arrogantly pressuring Vietnam to curtail its relationship with its beloved Soviet Union, and abandoning the precious socialism it so highly valued. Viewing itself in rather grandiose terms, Hanoi sought to establish Vietnam as a model for third world development, with equal if not greater appeal to developing nations than anything China could offer. Far from the student/teacher relationship envisioned by China, Vietnam saw its relationship with China as one of equals, in which Vietnam's ties with the Soviet Union would balance the proximity and power of its ancient nemesis.

Such wishful thinking, however, was no substitute for sound policy. As efforts to eradicate the elusive Khmer Rouge dragged into years, Vietnam found itself estranged from international support and faced with a costly confrontation on its China border. Vietnam also witnessed the increasing prosperity that China derived from its economic reforms.[5] Facing extreme poverty, it resolved, in 1987, to quit Cambodia. A year later, it undertook a "multidirectional" foreign policy that was to include reconciliation with China, close interaction with the Association of Southeast Asian Nations (ASEAN), and a major opening to the international community.[6] Coupled with the *doi moi* (renovation) policy announced at the sixth party congress in 1986, these changes provided strong evidence that Vietnam was setting a new course. From 1988 to 1990 Chinese and Vietnamese officials explored normalization, and in 1991 they reestablished diplomatic relations.[7]

Although improvement in Sino-Vietnamese relations in the 1990s proceeded slowly, Vietnam gradually reverted to a deferential attitude toward its northern neighbor. As a Vietnamese official recently remarked, "Remember after defeating the Chinese we always sent tribute."[8] By the end of the decade, Vietnamese leaders were flocking to Beijing, typically replete with platitudes extolling the virtues of the Chinese political or economic system, marking not only reconciliation with their giant neighbor, but also recognition of Chinese superiority in an unequal relationship that overshadows all others.

The Policy Change

What forces drove Vietnam to such an apparently extreme turnaround in its policy toward China, and do they represent, as the Vietnamese official put it, a repetition of historical Vietnamese tributary status? The answer to these questions is complex, but certain factors appear to have impelled the change. First, the Vietnamese leadership appears to have made the assessment that (a) China's market socialism is the wave of the future, and (b) Chinese military power is ascendant in Asia.[9] In this view, Hanoi sees a need to accommodate to the rising power of China and therefore has decided to do so sooner rather than later, while it still retains negotiating leverage.

A second explanation is that Vietnam, after joining ASEAN and normalizing relations with the United States in 1995, became somewhat disenchanted with both. The Asian financial crisis of 1997–98, instability in Indonesia, and the inability of ASEAN to act in concert with respect to the South China Sea all reduced the status of ASEAN among key Vietnamese leaders. Meanwhile, U.S. trade and investment, as shown in chapter 5, lagged behind that of nearly every major Asian nation and brought with it a stated U.S. intention of moving Vietnam toward democracy, castigated by the leadership as a plot for "peaceful evolution."

Third, Vietnam's China policy is explained in terms of the need for stability. The view in Hanoi is that without stability there can be no economic development and without China there can be no stability. The high price Vietnam paid to maintain troops in Cambodia and simultaneously confront China will not be repeated. Economic development has become the principal legitimizing factor for the regimes in both China and Vietnam, and Hanoi can ill afford to risk it with a destabilizing China policy.[10] The way in which Vietnam relates to China is crucial to this stability. By accepting the position of little brother, Vietnam has effectively neutralized Chinese animosities deriving from Vietnam's postwar challenge to China's "rightful place" in Asia. The structure of the relationship approximates that of the traditional one-nation-dominant concept presented by Hans Morgenthau as one of several systems favoring stable international relations.[11]

Fourth, and closely related to the goal of maintaining stability, Vietnam has sought to settle its border problems with China as best it can before Chinese power grows to the point where any agreement would be reached only on terms even more advantageous to China. While this subject is discussed elsewhere in this study, the point here is that Vietnam believes that its negotiating position will weaken over time because it perceives China moving further and further ahead in economic and military power. It is for this reason, among others, that Vietnam agreed to the land border agreement at the end of 1999, and it is also for this reason that Vietnam is putting its best face on the agreement reached with China in the Tonkin Gulf, despite having to cede significant sea areas that it had previously claimed were indisputably Vietnamese.[12]

Before the Tonkin Gulf agreement, a Vietnamese official described Hanoi's concern thusly: "We hope to settle the Gulf of Tonkin issue by end of the year 2000. Such a settlement is important not just for Vietnam, but also for peace and stability in Southeast Asia and the region." The same official, however, pointed to difficulty in achieving agreements on the rest of the South China Sea, stating that "Chinese activity in the South China Sea is driven by a desire to have a pressure point at which to influence Southeast Asia in the future."[13]

While all these reasons for a change of heart in Hanoi are plausible, the most important reason for the change, by far, is the identification of the Communist Party of Vietnam with that of China. Maintaining the regime has become an overarching goal of both states. Although both parties rose to power by capturing the mantle of nationalism, their legitimacy today is primarily a function of the relative success of their "socialist market economies." As described in chapter 5, those economies are under stress today, marked by declining growth rates and rising unemployment. At the same time, the political leadership in both countries is seen as increasingly corrupt, bureaucratic, and unable to cope with modernization. Under these circumstances, "it was only natural that the two largest remaining Leninist states would cling to one another to perpetuate their political systems and protect their power against the forces of globalization and the democratization process."[14]

Vietnamese Dependency

As the Communist parties governing China and Vietnam came under stress, they increasingly turned to each other for political support. Thus we see, at the turn of the century, a crescendo of dialogue between the two parties as well as between their respective mass organizations.

The February 1998 meeting between Vietnamese Communist Party general secretary Le Kha Phieu and his Chinese counterpart, Jiang

Zemin, set the tone for subsequent meetings. Before his departure for Beijing, Phieu was quoted as saying, "I would like to seize the opportunity of my trip to study China's precious experiences in building socialism with Chinese identity."[15]

On 23 February Jiang hosted Phieu at the Great Hall of the People. During the meeting, the two leaders defined the relationship to which they aspired for the twenty-first century. In the realm of security, they emphasized settlement of outstanding border and sea disputes and the nonuse of force to settle them. In a practical sense, this meant Vietnam's striking the best agreement it possibly could, while dealing from a weak hand.[16] (See chapter 4.) On the economic front, they stressed the benefits of greater trade and Chinese assistance to Vietnam, again with Vietnam playing the role of supplicant. (See chapter 5.) Finally, on a political plane, they emphasized the leading role of their Communist parties in promoting socialism.

While both leaders emphasized good neighborliness and pledged "comprehensive cooperation between the two parties and nations," the Vietnamese party chairman again played the role of student to teacher and was quoted as praising the Chinese model of socialism and repeating that he "saw with his own eyes" the tremendous achievements made by China.[17] The asymmetric nature of the relationship was even highlighted in statements of common goals, as the Chinese pointed out that the two nations are "joined by common mountains and rivers and that exchanges between the two countries go back to ancient times."[18]

Although this latter point could be interpreted as a statement of goodwill, it clearly conveys the message that Vietnam cannot escape its geographic and historical dependence on China. There is thus an indication, in the Phieu-Jiang summit, of Hanoi acknowledging the military, economic, and political superiority of China in a way reminiscent of the tributary status Vietnam had toward China for a thousand years.

Subsequent visits by Vietnamese leaders to China reinforce this conclusion. Although annual pilgrimages to Beijing had already become part of the ritual of the relationship before the Phieu visit, the number accelerated dramatically as the century ended. Formal exchanges at the vice minister level and above increased from 52 in 1998 to 80 in 1999.[19] The following are typical of the deferential attitude of Vietnamese

leaders in these exchanges. They also emphasize the overarching importance of economic success as legitimizing the role of their respective
parties.

- In April 1999 the Chinese Peoples Political Consultative Conference (CPPCC) and the Vietnam Motherland Front, both mass
  organizations to support party policies, held a joint conference
  in the Great Hall of the People. The Vietnamese side paid homage
  to "China's tremendous and profound changes," saying they
  learned about "the successful experiences of the party and government of China in economic development and in the work of
  China's CPPCC."[20]
- In August 1999 the Vietnam Fatherland Front hosted the same
  organization at its national congress in Hanoi. Both sides praised
  the success of their parties in buffering their countries from the
  effects of the Asian economic crisis.[21]
- In October 1999 Chinese Politburo Standing Committee member Li Ruihuan told his Vietnamese counterpart, Pham The
  Duyet, that the great achievement of China's reform is a lesson for
  Vietnam about the triumph of Marxism, "a general truth . . . by
  which mankind can rebuild the world."[22]
- In January 2000 China and Vietnam celebrated the 50th anniversary of China's extension of diplomatic relations to Vietnam.
  Vietnam expressed profound gratitude at the time, but China
  continued to remind Vietnam of its historic dependence on
  Chinese recognition throughout the year.[23]
- In February 2000 Nguyen Dy Nien, newly appointed as Vietnamese foreign minister, immediately visited China, his first visit
  outside the country. Nien met with his Chinese counterpart,
  Tang Jiaxuan, as well as with Premier Zhu Rongji, who said the
  visit "clearly shows the Vietnamese party and government attach
  great importance to the development of Sino-Vietnamese
  relations."[24]
- In June 2000 the Chinese Academy of Social Sciences, led by
  Chinese Politburo member Li Tingyie, hosted a theoretical semi-
  nar on economic reform for Vietnamese Politburo member Nguyen Duc Binh and a 16-member delegation from Vietnam. The

focus of the meeting was how to reform a socialist economy and still retain party political control. Organized at the request of Vietnamese party general secretary Le Kha Phieu, the session illustrated once again a Vietnam kowtowing to China in its attitude. "If China succeeds in its reform then we'll succeed, if China fails, we fail," said Phieu. The Vietnamese delegation then traveled to southwest China for a field session on economic reform.[25]

- In April 2000 Nong Duc Manh, chairman of the Vietnam's National Assembly, visited Beijing, paying similar obeisance, as did President Tran Duc Luong a few months later.[26]

- In July 2000 Vietnamese Politburo member Nguyen Minh Triet visited Beijing "to learn from China's experiences."

- In September 2000 Vietnamese prime minister Phan Van Khai held meetings with Chinese president Jiang Zemin, telling him Vietnam would like to "learn from China's experiences in economic development."[27]

- At their ninth party congress in April 2001, Vietnamese Communist Party leaders paid strong tribute to visiting dignitary Hu Jintao, vice president and member of the Standing Committee of the Communist Party of China. Hu had a visible role at the congress, praising Vietnam for adhering to Marxist-Leninist thought and keeping "firmly to the path of socialism." He stressed that promoting Sino-Vietnamese cooperation served their common socialist cause. Vietnamese leaders reciprocated with praise of China and stressed the closeness of their party-to-party and state-to-state relations.[28]

Vietnam's dependence on China was further manifested in the nature of the dialogue between the parties. For example, in 1998 Vietnam postponed the sixth party congress plenum so that Premier Phan Van Khai could visit China at a time convenient to the Chinese.[29] Likewise, although outstanding issues remained unresolved in the Tonkin Gulf, Chinese party leaders throughout the year 2000 constantly reminded their Vietnamese visitors of the need to reach an agreement by the end of the year.

The External Search for Alternatives

Although the official Vietnamese position and attitude toward China is deferential, this view by no means represents the totality of Vietnamese attitudes about the proper relationship it should have with its neighbor.

One dimension of that relationship has to do with security. Those concerned with a potential Chinese threat recall the 1979 invasion and fear future confrontations with China in the South China Sea. A close observer of Vietnam for many years has stated it thusly: "The rifts are between those in the military and security branches of government who see China as the country's last remaining socialist friend, and those in the Foreign Ministry, as well as many academics, who point to the threat China could pose in 10 years' time as it builds up its military strength, especially the navy."[30]

While this assessment reflects real attitudes, there is a great deal of rhetoric and activity these days about friendship between the People's Liberation Army (PLA) and the People's Army of Vietnam (PAVN). Defense ministers and generals regularly exchange visits.[31] The Vietnamese defense minister, for example, recently attended a reception commemorating the founding of the PLA.[32] Chinese troops gained some goodwill by working from the end of 1997 for nearly two years to clean up a reported half million landmines and 180,000 explosive traps strewn by both Vietnam and China during their border war of 1979.[33] The PLA and the PAVN share a commonality of missions as purported bastions against peaceful evolution, with both militaries stressing party control, and both reporting that vigilance is required against "hostile forces" plotting to undermine socialism.[34] Both countries also sharply cut the size of their military forces.[35]

For its part, the military in Vietnam remains suspicious of China. Remembering the 1979 war with clarity, a senior Vietnamese military officer recently stated that Beijing's intention was to reestablish imperial control of Vietnam as a father would control his children. Another officer said that China had a long-held view of Vietnam as "an impudent child on its southern boundary," and that Beijing sought to assert deeply held Chinese views of its suzerainty over Vietnam. With regard to the warming trend in current Sino-Vietnamese politics, he quoted an ancient Chinese proverb, "The coldness of a single day cannot make three feet deep a frozen river."[36] PAVN officers are also concerned about potential Chinese pressure against Vietnamese positions in the South China Sea. As indicated by their fortification of a significant number of islets, increased purchases of Russian naval craft and equipment, and maintenance of a large ready reserve, the PAVN remains nervous about long-term Chinese intentions. It thus appears that the oft-stated differences on China between the military and civilian sectors of Vietnamese society are overdrawn.

Of even greater importance, however, are the political rifts between those who see an opportunity to exploit the alternatives available for Vietnam resulting from the end of the colonial era, as stated earlier. This viewpoint is most clearly reflected in recent Vietnamese efforts to establish an omnidirectional foreign policy. For example, in his closing remarks to foreign guests attending the ninth party congress, the new Vietnamese party general secretary, Nong Duc Manh, emphasized that Vietnam was seeking to pursue a multidirectional foreign policy for Vietnam, with "diversification of international relations."[37]

Foremost in this effort is building a constructive relationship with ASEAN. Vietnam joined ASEAN in 1995. A major motivation for the move was economic, as 60 percent of Vietnamese foreign trade was already with ASEAN nations that year, and membership promised to expand that trade significantly. By joining the ASEAN Free Trade Area, Vietnam also promised to open its economy by 2006, a clear objective of reformers such as former premier Vo Van Kiet. Vietnam also undoubtedly understood that it could benefit from its association with ASEAN in any confrontation in the South China Sea. In fact, Hanoi did seek and receive the private support of some ASEAN countries in its efforts to have a Chinese oil rig removed from the Vietnamese-claimed exclusive economic zone in the Tonkin Gulf in 1997. Finally, joining ASEAN provided Vietnam a means of demonstrating its international openness, making it more attractive to international donors and investors. Vietnam fully expected that its ASEAN orientation would, at a minimum, divorce it from its increasing reliance on China.[38]

Hanoi's turn toward ASEAN, however, stimulated concerns among party cadre about its affect on Vietnam's political evolution. Former Politburo member Dao Duy Tung and former party general secretary Do Muoi began by warning of the dangers attending too close a relationship with capitalist countries.[39] Seizing on the difficult conditions facing ASEAN because of the upheaval in Indonesia and the Asian economic crisis, their successors, Politburo member Pham The Duyet and general secretary Le Kha Phieu, sounded a similar refrain. With due respect to the sensitivities of China, Vietnamese leaders since 1995 have hastened to assure China that its window to ASEAN in no way signifies a deprecation of its relationship with China. Instead, Hanoi has emphasized its intention to cooperate with China with respect to ASEAN and to support Beijing's policy of expanding the Chinese relationship with ASEAN.[40]

Chinese concern about Vietnam's direction, however, was temporarily allayed in 1997 and 1998 as ASEAN struggled to contend with the Asian economic crisis. China took the opportunity to emphasize that the socialist countries of Asia were not responsible for the crisis and that China was prepared to assist Vietnam in weathering the economic storm. In 1997 it initiated the ASEAN-China Joint Cooperation Committee with the stated purpose of improving dialogue with the ASEAN states. Both in annual sessions of the committee and in other forums China courted the favor of its ASEAN neighbors by assisting with highly visible aid projects and emphasizing its benevolence in not devaluing its currency.[41] China further negotiated long-term agreements with Vietnam, Thailand, Brunei, and Malaysia that included a declaration of principles based on the United Nations Charter, the Five Principles of Peaceful Coexistence, and the Treaty of Amity and Cooperation in Southeast Asia.

As it developed its relationship with ASEAN, China sought to influence the organization in several ways. First, it sought ASEAN support for a one-China policy, which it gained in principle at the Sixth ASEAN Regional Forum (ARF) in July 1999.[42] Second, it supported a regional nuclear-free zone, becoming the first nuclear weapon state to subscribe to the Southeast Asia Nuclear Weapon Free Zone Treaty.[43] Third, it supported, albeit with caveats, confidence-building measures in the South China Sea. Fourth, it initiated defense cooperation with several states, including Myanmar (Burma), Thailand, the Philippines, and Singapore.[44] Fifth, it lobbied to ensure that ASEAN does not evolve into a military bloc.[45] Most important for China, however, was its effort to develop a relationship with ASEAN that excluded the United States. In so doing China stressed multipolarity, but emphasized that the best approach to resolve outstanding issues was through the ASEAN-plus-three (China, Japan, and South Korea) grouping. In all these manners,

China influenced ASEAN in a way that would, inter alia, minimize the opportunity for Vietnam to turn to ASEAN as an alternative for its most important relationship, that with China.

Some Vietnamese, however, look not to ASEAN or China, but to Taiwan, as a model for future development. There are over 500 Taiwan businessmen permanently living in Vietnam.[46] Taiwan is Vietnam's second largest cumulative investor, third largest source of imports, and fourth largest export market.[47] Moreover, as indicated in chapter 5, many Vietnamese economists and academics see a parallel between Taiwan and Vietnam, as Taiwan evolved from an agricultural economy with authoritarian leadership into a diversified modern economy with democratic rule. Afraid to speak up for fear of upsetting the leadership, these individuals work with more modest reform packages they think are possible in today's Vietnam. Meanwhile, nearly all Vietnamese support the one-China principle, including noninterference by outside powers (that is, the United States), although for reasons previously cited about the military, there is likely some apprehension about China's actually taking over Taiwan. One indication of the tension over Taiwan is an episode that occurred on the last day of 1998, when Vietnam announced that Taiwan goods would henceforth be subject to ordinary tariffs. The move, designed to restrict burgeoning Taiwan trade and investment, did not set well with Vietnamese entrepreneurs, who complained vociferously to the board of trade. Two days later most-favored-nation (now permanent normal trade relations) treatment was reinstated.[48]

Dwindling but still significant numbers of the Vietnamese elite continue to look to Russia as a major power to balance China. In 1999 Russian defense minister Igor Sergeyev and his Vietnamese counterpart, Pham Van Tra, signed an agreement on military-to-military technical cooperation. Russia supplies Vietnam with Su-27 aircraft and Tarantul-class naval craft and is planning to upgrade Vietnam's MiG aircraft fleet. It has trained more than 13,000 Vietnamese specialists, and, although it no longer maintains significant naval forces in Vietnam, it retains access to Cam Ranh Bay under an agreement that lasts until 2004.[49] Russia also donates considerable aid to Vietnam and provides the technology and capital to make Vietsovpetro (Petro Vietnam and Zarubezneft) Vietnam's most profitable offshore enterprise. Russian president Vladimir Putin visited Vietnam in March 2001 to solidify an eroding security and economic relationship, seeking to add to the aforementioned list of arms supply contracts. Many observers were skeptical. For example, Moscow radio reported: "Vietnam really wants to buy something from us. The trouble is that they have no money."[50] On the political front, moreover, Russia generally fails the test, because Vietnamese leaders, with Chinese encouragement, see Russian political reform as a disaster.[51]

While looking to Europe, Japan, and Korea as major economic partners, many Vietnamese see the United States as the most attractive alternative to the present reliance on China. Searching for political stability during a time of rapid technological and cultural change, these Vietnamese view the United States as a model that in some respects may surpass that of China. For example, party veterans still acknowledge the importance of Ho Chi Minh's declaration of independence in August 1945, a text patterned almost exactly after that of the American Declaration of Independence. His opening words were, "All men are created equal. They are endowed by their Creator with certain inalienable rights; among these are life, liberty, and the pursuit of happiness."[52] There is also no question that the economic attractiveness of the United States surpasses that of China.

Nevertheless, party leaders frequently refer to their fears that U.S. influence may lead to "peaceful evolution" away from Communist Party rule. Indeed, they also fear the reaction of their counterpart party comrades in China, as they slowly proceed in developing their U.S. relationship. It has been reported that they therefore delayed the Vietnam-United States Trade Agreement, initialed by both sides in July 1999, until well after China gained U.S. approval of entry into the World Trade Organization (WTO).[53] Likewise, they twice postponed scheduled visits by the U.S. defense secretary, first in January 1999 because of the China summit between Le Kha Phieu and Jiang Zemin in February, and again in September 1999, because of support for the Chinese position on the U.S. attack on the PRC embassy in Belgrade. When the visit finally did occur in the summer of 2000, General Secretary Le Kha Phieu made a secret visit to Beijing to reassure China that nothing had changed in their strategic relationship.[54]

In conclusion, while Vietnam remains motivated to look elsewhere to diversify its economic, political, and military relationships, concern for China restricts interaction with the three prime objects of that search—ASEAN, Taiwan, and the United States. A Vietnamese official summarized his country's position as follows:

> We are always ready to negotiate with all countries, including China. To maintain good relations with China, Vietnam needs to negotiate. We think that normalization with both the United States and China has helped the situation. Joining ASEAN has also helped. We are a friend to all nations. We have fought so many wars and now want peace. We need it for development. We now have diplomatic relations with over 150 countries, but we still need to treat our big neighbor in a special way. We are flexible in our negotiations with the PRC. We recognize the relationship is one of a major power to a small power. Nevertheless, we will defend our sovereignty. We need and want development. This requires peace. We need to contribute to that peace. We also want a China that develops successfully and is peaceful and friendly. We do not want major powers making compromises at our expense. This is the lesson of the 20th century. We hope the 21st century will bring better relations with China and the United States, but we want no compromises at our expense.[55]

The Internal Search for Alternatives

While official delegations sing the praises of the Chinese political and economic system, a significant search for alternative answers to internal development is under way in Vietnam. Much of the sound and fury in the internal debate centers on economic policy, but the root cause of Vietnam's discontent is fear that the Chinese model may be a blind alley. Indeed, Duong Thu Huong, the famous (or infamous, if you are a party member) Vietnamese writer who served eight years with the PAVN in South Vietnam, has labeled Vietnam just that—a paradise of the blind.[56] Her four novels, for which she was imprisoned for a couple years in Hanoi, stand as a stark condemnation of party efforts to rebuild a new and more humane society in Vietnam after the war. She is not alone. In 1999, at the second session of the party Central Committee, a member invited Nguyen Duc Binh, the ideology chief, to visit the poor of the Central Highlands and explain how Marxism-Leninism could feed them.[57]

General Tran Do, former chief of ideology of the party's Commission for Culture, Literature, and the Arts, and a Central Committee member, repeatedly condemned the fundamental premise upon which current party doctrine rests, the Chinese line of tight central political control while allowing very modest market reform: "Do we need a developed country with enough food and clothes, freedom and happiness—i.e., democracy . . . or do we need a country with socialist orientation that is very poor?"[58] Expelled from the party in January 1999 after calling on it to "reform or die," General Do nevertheless stands as a symbol of resistance to the rigid doctrine emanating from Hanoi at the turn of the century. He has been defended by numerous party members, including former Haiphong party secretary Lieutenant General Pham Hong Son, who was arrested for his protests, and who, while still under arrest in March 2000, circulated a paper on "the Soviet-style boot camp society" of Vietnam.[59]

As indicated earlier, Vietnamese in many walks of life have called for an end to the corruption that, as in China, has become so pervasive. According to the Vietnamese Communist Party, during the last 30 months of the 1990s, its inspection committees received complaints about 18,000 party members, mostly about corruption, with "70 percent guilty and disciplined."[60] Many of the sons and daughters of rich party members are seen as corrupt, morally depraved, and without social responsibility.[61]

Abuses by senior party members are becoming common and led to major riots in Thai Binh Province in 1997–98. Although the government placated the protestors by removing some corrupt provincial leaders, discontent remains below the surface. Small demonstrations erupted in Hanoi, Nha Trang, and Ho Chi Minh City in the fall of 2000.[62] Newspaper personnel who question the system that spawns such corruption are arrested.[63] Prime Minister Phan Van Khai reportedly tendered his resignation in protest to the selective nature of the crackdown on corruption.[64]

Although not quite as pervasive, Vietnamese corruption closely follows the pattern of China, involving both local officials and party members. The recent revelation of massive corruption in Fujian Province, involving over $3 billion in illegal transactions, shows just one example of how deeply corruption has taken hold in major Chinese localities. The following report illustrates its pervasiveness.

Xiamen, one of China's wealthiest port cities, did not have just a
handful of senior officials on the take. A shady local businessman
methodically bought off representatives of almost every arm of the
state, including the local Communist Party committee, the customs
administration, the police and even, if popular reports are to be
believed, the local bureau of the Ministry of State Security and the
People's Armed Police.[65]

Not only has corruption in Vietnam been strikingly similar to that
in China, but also the reaction to it by both regimes has been nearly
identical. Vietnam, like China, has manifested heightened intolerance
toward dissidents. At the eighth plenum of the eighth VCP Central
Committee congress in November 1999, the regime focused on rooting
out corruption and dissidents, just as the fifteenth Chinese party congress did in 1997.[66] Both regimes conduct periodic anticorruption
campaigns that officially target corrupt members but that also attack
dissidents. Just as China conducts rectification campaigns, Vietnam
recently concluded a two-year purification campaign, designed to root
out evil influences in the party.[67]

Both regimes also attempt to co-opt local opposition by appointing
loyal Party cadres the leadership of the People's Committees of their
provinces and districts.[68] Both send promising young loyalists to indoc-
trination sessions at provincial and national party headquarters. Both
aspire to control the reform process from the center, thereby maintaining
the power to reap for the party and for themselves the economic benefits
of reform while limiting its potential for creating competing interest
groups.[69] In effect, both regimes seek to maintain their own power
base, including the wealth generated by economic reforms, while justifying that power base in terms of legitimacy derived from leadership of
their respective nationalist movements during the twentieth century.

The Vietnamese search for alternatives to the Chinese political and
economic model, therefore, carries implications challenging the very
foundations of party legitimacy. While realists in the party acknowledge
the corruption and the growing popular apathy and cynicism toward
the system, they are afraid to speak out for fear of being purged in the
current purification campaign.[70] The result is party and governmental
paralysis, with emulators of the Chinese political and economic system
pitted against reformers who see value in some of the economic reforms

in China but who emphasize reforms that disperse decision-making authority to the provinces and the private sector.

Nowhere is this divide more apparent than in the attitude toward the state-owned enterprises (SOEs). While Vietnamese reformers have been trying to limit the economic power and influence of the SOEs for years, their efforts have been largely thwarted. Governmental plans to reduce the number of SOEs to 3,000 from 5,500 are moving slowly, with only 370 companies equitized (privatized) by the beginning of 2000.[71] As in China, most SOEs are heavily in debt, with many virtually bankrupt. They absorb 70 to 75 percent of all domestic lending by the four major state-owned banks, which, like their Chinese counterparts, are very weak. Despite repeated urging by the World Bank and the International Monetary Fund, Hanoi clings to the security blanket of state-run industries, citing the reputed success of China as justification.[72] Deputy Prime Minister Nguyen Tan Dung had promised a drastic overhaul of SOEs, but former General Secretary Phieu continued to support them, and even wanted to strengthen them.

A final internal area where Vietnam could diverge from the Chinese model is adaptation to the information revolution. Again, for reasons of control, Vietnam follows the Chinese model. China remains reluctant to embrace the information technology revolution, recently barring foreign companies from assigning Chinese language web addresses to web sites in China, and issuing new regulations to control information on the Internet.[73]

In negotiating for U.S. approval of its entrance into the WTO, the Chinese minister of information industry, Wu Jichuan, told the media there would be no significant effect of the WTO on China's information industry and he would strengthen his supervisory functions.[74] He had resisted foreign participation in the Internet and the telecom industry, but after WTO accession, foreign investment in the Chinese Internet is supposed to be allowed.[75] Likewise, information control is paramount in Vietnam. Information technology access was launched only in December 1997, and the Vietnam Ministry of Post and Telecommunications has kept control of the international gateway. As of early 2000, computers in the network were restricted to only 60,000 students, and even there the access costs were unaffordable for 95 percent of the students.[76]

The Relationship in Perspective

There are numerous practical areas where improved Sino-Vietnamese relations have benefited both countries. Without the risk of land conflict, both sides can divert to other uses the type of resources they spent for over a decade in beefing up their border forces.

Trade has increased markedly, and although it is a mixed blessing from Vietnam's perspective, it probably is a net plus. Rail links were restored in 1996. Mail service has been restored. Bridges, such as the newly constructed one over the Nam Thi River between Lao Cai and Hekou, facilitate trade and exchanges. Chinese tourism, which soared from 19,000 in 1995 to over 600,000 in 2001, adds to Vietnam's foreign exchange.[77]

In 1999 China completed clearing hundreds of thousands of landmines in Vietnam, and in 2000 it provided relief to flood victims along Vietnam's central coast. These and other practical measures to benefit their citizens are a consequence of a peaceful relationship that has begun to develop where mistrust and conflict has too often held sway. All this is good for Vietnam.

The problem for Vietnam is that the relationship has been developing as an unequal one. Insofar as China has 28 times the land area and 15 times the population of Vietnam, the relationship will never be symmetrical. But this does not mean that Vietnam must allow the Chinese line to dominate its domestic and international orientation. Throughout history Vietnam has sought to assert its independence from China. It was largely successful in its effort when the Middle Kingdom was weak, but when it was strong, as China is today, Vietnam felt Chinese pressure. Vietnamese leaders sought investiture from and paid tribute to the Chinese court, not unlike the pilgrimages Vietnamese leaders make to Beijing immediately after their appointment to high positions today. Sinicization followed, just as the Chinese brand of socialism drives much of the Vietnamese economic and social system today.[78] But by following the Chinese pattern of concentrating power in the hands of the imperial court and the mandarins, Vietnam opened itself to corruption and abuses, just as the total political control by the Communist Party of Vietnam tends to do today.

As the pattern of abuses led to rebellion in the past, popular apathy and discontent today are a warning for tomorrow. But they are a warning not just to the party, but also to the poor people of Vietnam who have had, for centuries, to struggle with Chinese invasions in support of corrupt but loyalist Vietnamese regimes.[79]

As Vietnam enters a new century and a new millenium, the opportunities to break this vicious cycle of history are manifold. International trade, investment, and assistance are available today in quantities inconceivable in earlier times. International exchanges and communication, capital flows, and scientific and technology transfer are the hallmarks of the new century. Geographic proximity, while important, is no longer the dominant theme of modern international relations. Japan and China trade more with the United States than does Mexico. France invests more in Vietnam than does China. So too, Vietnam may find models of political development, such as Taiwan or the United States, more relevant to its future than that of China. The leadership in Hanoi is beginning to realize this. They say that they want an omnidirectional foreign policy, in which they do not want to be part of any major power alliance system. But their concern for maintaining the party as the sole source and arbiter of political power obscures their vision of what Vietnam could become—a Vietnam that leads, not follows, China in the twenty-first century. Such a Vietnam would need a multifaceted agenda of political and economic reform that fulfills earlier party promises to serve as an example for third world development. The model for such an agenda is to be found not in Beijing, but in the gradual transformation to democracy among its successful Asian neighbors.

CHAPTER 7

American Interests and the Future of Sino-Vietnamese Relations

A generation ago, the United States fought a war in Indochina in large part to contain perceived Sino-Soviet expansionism in Asia. U.S. policymakers then believed that China was seeking a sphere of influence in Southeast Asia by supporting Communist insurgencies therein. In this view, China was using Vietnam as a test case for "wars of national liberation," not only for Southeast Asia, but also for the rest of the developing world. The U.S. position was not new. During the early 1950s, U.S. aid to French Indochina was justified as countering Chinese-supported aggression and offsetting Chinese military aid to the Viet Minh.[1] During the early 1960s, the United States justified its logistical and advisory support for the Republic of Vietnam as a way of containing Chinese-supported wars of aggression. In 1965 President Lyndon Johnson explained his decision to commit U.S. troops in South Vietnam in terms of a "Jakarta-Hanoi-Beijing-Pyongyang axis, with Cambodia probably to be brought in as a junior partner and Laos to be merely absorbed by the North Vietnamese and the Chinese."[2] American leaders became especially concerned after Chinese defense minister Lin Piao delivered his famous treatise, "Long Live the Victory of People's War," in which he called for the "countryside" of the world (China and other third world areas) to isolate and overwhelm the "cities" of the world (the United States and Western Europe).

Today the Lin Piao paradigm appears particularly ironic, as the people of the "countryside" in China, and to a more limited extent in Vietnam, increasingly express discontent with their Communist Party leadership, while the "cities" of the world, represented by their economic and information products, spread across national boundaries on a global basis. The U.S. fear of domino nations falling to or for Communist leadership has, to a large degree, been replaced by confidence that the socioeconomic progress of those "dominos" represents a challenge to the ideology and leadership of Beijing and Hanoi, even to the point where a reverse domino effect may be possible.

Under such circumstances, the U.S. interest in Sino-Vietnamese relations has altered dramatically. The importance of Vietnam as attested to by the names of 59,000 U.S. servicemen on the Vietnam Memorial in the nation's capital is no more. Vietnam is seen largely as a historical artifact by the Vietnam generation, or a great place for backpacking by the X generation. Once again, most Americans cannot locate Vietnam on a map and policymakers see it as a backwater of Asia, without any particular strategic or economic significance.

In contrast, U.S. leaders view China as extremely important for the future of the United States. Its 1.25 billion people, status as a nuclear power, growing economic strength, and potential to affect stability in Asia and the world all make China a nation to be reckoned with.

Asymmetry exists, therefore, not only in the relationship between China and Vietnam, but also between U.S. interests and policy toward China, and U.S. interests and policy toward Vietnam. In any geopolitical calculation, the future of the relationship between China and Vietnam is important to the United States principally insofar as it is likely to affect Sino-U.S. relations.

That reality, however, does not alter the possibility that the United States might influence the future of Sino-Vietnamese relations through either Beijing or Hanoi. In so doing, two questions come immediately to mind. Why should the United States care what transpires between these two Asian Communist states, and if it does care, how can it influence that relationship so that it coincides more closely with U.S. interests in Asia and the world? Despite the relative insignificance of Vietnam in current U.S. foreign policy, this chapter argues that the United States can take initiatives that have a modest chance of influencing very significant changes in the future direction of both countries. If successful, the initiatives would benefit not only U.S interests, but also the long-term development of both China and Vietnam.

Current U.S. Policy and Sino-Vietnamese Relations

Improvements in U.S. relations with Vietnam have not kept pace with those with China. The sporadic support for full normalization with Vietnam has been caused in part by Vietnam's slowness in providing information on missing U.S. servicemen, but also by its slowness in instituting real economic and political reform. After establishing diplomatic relations in 1995, Washington did not post an ambassador to Hanoi until 1997. It initialed a bilateral trade agreement (BTA) in 1999, but it did not sign it until a year later, and only ratified it in late 2001.[3] U.S. companies, meanwhile, continue to cut back plans for increased trade and investment because of bureaucratic and legal obstacles in doing business in Vietnam.

By way of comparison, the United States normalized relations with China 16 years before doing so with Vietnam. It granted most-favored-nation treatment to China over 20 years before doing the same to Vietnam. U.S. businesses conduct over 80 times more trade with China than with Vietnam. Even before the Clinton administration sent the BTA, which included nonpermanent normal trade relations with Vietnam, to the Congress, the House and Senate had already approved permanent normal trade relations with China. Despite a relatively poorer Chinese record on human rights and political and religious freedom, and despite Chinese actions contrary to U.S. objectives in which Vietnam is not engaged, such as missile proliferation and threats against Taiwan, U.S. policy is clearly more accommodating to China than it is to Vietnam.

Likewise, Vietnam is clearly more accommodating to China than to the United States. This fact was well illustrated in the long delay in consummating the BTA. When the agreement was first announced, President Clinton stated that the United States and Vietnam had reached a broad trade agreement that included normal trade relations with Vietnam.[4] Initialed in July 1999, the BTA would normally have been closed about three months later. However, Vietnam procrastinated in providing formal signature and tried to reopen the negotiations, even to the point of temporarily raising tariffs on U.S. goods in the hope of reaching a more favorable agreement. Although Hanoi indicated that it was prepared to sign the agreement at the Asia Pacific Economic Cooperation (APEC) summit in New Zealand in September 1999, Vietnamese representatives at the last minute declared that it was impossible to sign and that they would require more time to study it.[5] Even after the U.S. side said it would not reopen negotiations, the Vietnamese continued to press for changes, and in April 2000 made one last major effort to revise the agreement. Finally, in July 2000, Vietnam signed the agreement.

Vietnam's delay in signing the initialed agreement was a function of several factors, but avoiding irritation of China appeared to be a major consideration. The length and complexity of the BTA may also have been a factor, but the fact that Vietnamese negotiators had already initialed it demonstrates not misunderstanding, but disagreement among the top leadership in Hanoi about its relative costs and benefits. The benefits were rather clear. Vietnam would, by World Bank estimates, double its exports to the United States during the first full year of implementation and enjoy significant increases thereafter. Although Vietnamese exports to the United States were less than a billion dollars in 1999, the potential for growth is tremendous. BTA proponents pointed to increased foreign revenue as not only helping the sluggish economy, but also providing a major stimulus to long-term growth.[6] Moreover, it was a necessary first step in gaining entry into the World Trade Organization (WTO), providing greater opportunities to take advantage of the global economy.

Despite such compelling arguments, the leadership demurred. Hanoi was hoping to conclude the border agreement it finally reached with China at the end of 1999 and to settle the very difficult demarcation problem in the Tonkin Gulf in 2000. Moreover, BTA opponents felt that the agreement opened Vietnam too rapidly to U.S. influence. For example, some analysts believe that Secretary of State Madeleine Albright, by stressing human rights and democracy in her September 1999 visit, provided BTA opponents enough ammunition to delay the expected signing at the APEC summit later that month. In any case, Vietnam delayed signing until well after both its border agreements with China and U.S. approval of Chinese entry into the WTO (15 November 1999) were concluded.[7] While there is some debate over whether Chinese officials actually pressured Hanoi to delay the BTA, it is clear that the Vietnamese side acted in consideration of the effect of the agreement on its relations with China.

Current Chinese Concerns

An unexplored question is what influence negotiations over the BTA may have had on China. If Vietnamese calculations were correct, why would Chinese leaders be irritated if Vietnam entered into an agreement with the United States? What did they have to fear? Certainly the effect on China's minuscule trade with Vietnam was not a major concern. Did China see the BTA as reducing its influence on Vietnam? Did it fear that Vietnam might become less dependent on China? Would it force China to lower its trade barriers? Would it lead to political openness?

At the dawn of the new millennium, one thing clear to Beijing was that potential U.S. influence on Vietnam was already on the rise. The posting of a U.S. ambassador in 1997, the authorization of Overseas Private Investment Corporation and Export-Import Bank financial support in 1998 for U.S companies doing business with Vietnam, and the initialing of the BTA and the opening of the U.S. consulate in Saigon in 1999 may have caused China to take another look at the direction its southern neighbor was taking.[8]

Chinese actions and statements indicate three concerns with United States–Vietnam relations. First, the development of close U.S.-Vietnamese relations could undermine the Chinese policy of gaining increased influence in Southeast Asia. China interpreted the economic crisis of the late 1990s as an opportunity to assert its leadership in regional economic affairs. As shown in chapter 5, China made a major effort to portray itself as a benefactor to Vietnam, but this policy applied to the rest of Southeast Asia as well. Although China's role in the financial crisis was largely limited to its commitment not to devalue the renminbi, Beijing sought to demonstrate that it was its leadership in the region, to the exclusion of that of the United States, that was instrumental in solving the economic crisis. "I still advocate having Asia settle Asia's issues," Xu Dunxin, vice chairman of the National People's Congress Foreign Affairs Committee, was quoted as saying. China also joined with Vietnam in opposition to the United States in supporting the Southeast Asian Nuclear Weapons Free Zone.[9]

Second, any U.S. military-to-military relationship with Vietnam could legitimize the U.S. forward presence in Asia. In October 2000 China issued a White Paper on defense that criticized U.S. forward presence as unnecessary and destabilizing to the region.[10] This policy was in sharp contrast with previous Chinese recognition, in private meetings, of the stabilizing influence of U.S. military forces, especially with regard to preventing the militarization of Japan. In this context the unprecedented dispatch in 1999 of two USAF planes from Okinawa for flood relief in Vietnam provided unwelcome legitimacy to the U.S. military presence.[11] So too was the first postwar visit to Vietnam of a U.S. secretary of defense.

Secretary of Defense William Cohen was first scheduled to visit Vietnam in January 1999. Neither his visit that month nor a rescheduled visit for August that year ever materialized. The ostensible reason for the first postponement was that Vietnamese leaders were too busy. However, the real reason appears to have been that party leaders were afraid that the visit would cause problems for the all-important February 1999 summit between General Secretary Le Kha Phieu and his counterpart, Jiang Zemin.[12] January 1999 also marked the 49th anniversary of the establishment of diplomatic relations between China and Vietnam, an event that was marked by seminars and a diplomatic reception in both countries. Hanoi called off the second visit because it claimed the party was too busy with a campaign for reform.[13] Again, the real reason appears to have been a desire to support Chinese claims that the bombing of its embassy in Belgrade was a deliberate act and an example of U.S. interference in the internal affairs of other nations.[14] Cohen finally visited Vietnam in March 2000, but his talks were limited to MIAs and military cooperation in flood control and the medical field. The Vietnamese foreign ministry took pains to point out that any cooperation that developed would not be at the expense of China.[15]

In January 2001 Hanoi also canceled, at the last minute, a visit by the commander of U.S. Forces in the Pacific, Admiral Dennis Blair. Vietnam may have had many reasons for the cancellation, such as unrest in the Central Highlands, competing influences of party elites, and debate over the nature and extent of relations with the United States as they prepared for the ninth party congress in April. However, it is noteworthy that two months earlier Vietnam hosted a Chinese naval delegation that visited, among other places, Military Region Seven, which includes Cam Ranh Bay. According to reporting from Hanoi, a Vietnamese official stated that there could be no U.S. visit to Cam Ranh until China was invited first. U.S. ambassador Pete Peterson, however, stated, "we are not pressing for a ship visit. There is no urgency."[16] Nevertheless, the fact of the Chinese naval visit before Blair's scheduled visit, followed immediately afterward by the visit of the Chinese defense minister, indicates that Vietnam's "postponement" of Admiral Blair's visit may be tied to Chinese concern over Vietnamese cooperation with the U.S. military.[17]

Third and finally, U.S. influence on Vietnam could result in economic and political reforms that tend to undermine the legitimacy of the Communist Party of China. Every time the United States takes an initiative that would enhance its relationship with either China or Vietnam, the rhetoric from Washington focuses on how the steps taken will ultimately lead to greater political freedom in those countries.[18] Regardless of the possible contrasting views of the merits of that position, the fact is that Beijing is already nervous about its long-term ability to control events within its own borders. But while the Chinese Communist Party leadership has reason to believe it can control events in China, the same does not apply to Vietnamese Communist Party control in Vietnam. Thus, when former president Bill Clinton cited the promotion of democracy as a major reason for normalizing relations with Vietnam in 1995 and repeated that idea on the occasion of granting Vietnam normal trade relations in 2000, Beijing had every reason to worry that this U.S. policy would strike at the ideological foundations of its ruling Communist Party.[19] The official Chinese press thus took these occasions to criticize U.S. policy, as it did once again by publishing Le Kha Phieu's anti-American speech during the November 2000 Clinton visit.[20]

Future Sino-Vietnamese Relations: Four Scenarios

Future Sino-Vietnamese relations inevitably depend to some extent on the past. That past has been characterized by at least three types of relationships: conflict, alliance, and Vietnam as a tributary state to China. A fourth type of relationship, with Vietnam paying due respect to China but pursuing independent policies, has its origins in the past and could be a viable alternative in the future. These four types of relationships are at the core of possible scenarios that will affect and be affected by U.S. interests and policy in Asia.

The first is that of conflict. The type of open warfare both nations experienced in the past is the most obvious example, but an extended period of competition or disagreement over boundaries, resources, and national foreign and domestic policies is at the heart of this scenario. The most recent period epitomizing this type of relationship was the period from 1975 until 1991, during part of which mutual mistrust and suspicion actually erupted into open hostilities. Future conflict could be simply a series of local incidents, for example, a pattern of Chinese harassment and firing on Vietnamese fishing or patrol boats in the Gulf of Tonkin, or a more general conflict, such as Chinese attacks and seizure of Vietnamese-held features in the Spratly Islands.

The second is that of alliance. At various times during its long history, Vietnam used its close relationship with China to its advantage in contending with hostile powers. As a province of China during the first millennium A.D., it called on Chinese armies to defeat the aggression of neighboring Champa. More recently, it received vital Chinese support in the first and second Indochinese wars. In all these cases, the overriding imperative driving the alliance relationship appears to have been Vietnamese fear of domination by an outside power. More typical of past alliances, however, was Chinese support for a declining Vietnamese regime that was threatened from within. Such a scenario could recur if the regime in Hanoi falters in making needed reforms over an extended period, leading to civil unrest and an appeal for Chinese support to maintain the regime.

The third type of relationship is akin to the traditional Vietnamese tributary status with respect to China, in which Vietnam kowtows to its northern neighbor. This tributary relationship with China existed for nearly a thousand years, with Vietnamese delegations paying homage to the imperial Chinese court with varying degrees of intensity, most often directly correlated to the degree of political authority the dynasty then exercised. The tribute symbolically acknowledged the inferior status of Vietnam with respect to the Middle Kingdom. In this scenario, the inferior, Vietnam, would not take any major foreign or domestic policy initiatives that conflicted with the interests and policies of its superior, China. Although Vietnam is striving to maintain a degree of independence from China, the tone of recent Vietnamese delegations visiting China has begun to resemble this scenario.

The fourth possible scenario is what might be termed one of "due respect," in which Vietnam takes into account the interests of China but pursues independent foreign and domestic policies. Vietnam's historic southward movement, which was less dependent on Chinese acquiescence, presaged this type of relationship. In the modern era, an omnidirectional Vietnamese foreign policy that looks as much to the members of the Association of Southeast Asian Nations (ASEAN) and other nations as it does to China would be a primary characteristic of this scenario. The scenario would also see a Vietnam that pursues reforms that empower its people, from local village, district, and province councils to private entrepreneurs and interest groups.

Each of these scenarios can be analyzed in terms of the characteristics of the relationship described in previous chapters. These include national cultures of China and Vietnam, the degree of Vietnamese independence from China, the imbalance of their national power, disputes over the South China Sea, political ideology, regime maintenance, and economic benefit. Each of these characteristics tends to favor one or more of the above scenarios, as shown in table 7-1.

The popular and elite cultures of Vietnam and China are at variance. The elites of China and Vietnam have historic cultural ties that support two of the four scenarios listed: alliance and kowtow. Their common Confucian tradition of proper familial relationships extends to international relations, with obedience of the son to the father and deference from the younger brother to the older brother defining the nature of the relationship. Thus the leadership of both countries inherit a cultural tradition that tends to favor Vietnamese submission to China in exchange for Chinese benevolence and, if needed, protection of Vietnam against hostile outside forces. Conversely, popular Vietnamese culture, even though a beneficiary of Chinese culture, favors treating each person as part of the fabric of local society and working together for the common good. This attitude places Vietnamese interests first and foremost. It is closely linked to the second characteristic shaping future scenarios in Sino-Vietnamese relations—Vietnam's strong desire for independence.

Vietnam's love for independence, as it has on numerous occasions throughout history, could lead to conflict with China in the coming

Table 7-1: Which Factors Favor Each of the Four Scenarios?**

Factor → / Scenario ↳	National Culture*	National Independence	Relative National Power	S. China Sea Issues	Political Ideology	Regime Maintenance	Economic Benefit
Conflict	0 e, 0 p	+	0	+	0	0	–
Alliance	+ e, – p	0	+	–	+	+	0
Tribute	+ e, – p	–	+	+	+	+	–
Due respect	0 e, 0 p	+	0	+	0	0	+

** "+" indicates support for a particular scenario, "0" neutral or mixed support for it, and "–" opposition to it
* "e" indicates elite culture, and "p" popular culture

decades. Although Vietnam is recognized as an independent state by more than 150 nations, including China, disputes over Hanoi's exercise of sovereignty could arise. Should Vietnam establish alliances with a major power, seek hegemony in Indochina, or take military action to support its maritime claims, China would likely react, as it has in the past, with threat or use of force. The present government appears to recognize these realities and thus has avoided conflict. Future governments could do likewise, while expanding relations with ASEAN and other nations along the lines of the "due respect" scenario. In this case, relations with the United States would not develop into an alliance or an effort to contain China, but rather would be part of an overall Vietnamese policy of building strong economic and political ties with many nations.

The relative national power of China clearly favors either an alliance or a Vietnamese position of kowtowing to China. Hanoi's perception of China as a rising power in Asia is a strong factor in Vietnam's accommodating to Chinese interests. Hanoi would prefer an alliance with China if there were other outside forces threatening Vietnam's exercise of independence, but this is unlikely under current or conceivable international conditions. There exists, however, a real possibility that Vietnam could, as it has already begun to do, revert to the tributary relationship with China. If Hanoi sees Beijing commanding a stable political system, a dynamic economy, and an increasingly powerful People's Liberation Army (PLA), it will tend to emulate China and defer to it where there might be conflicting interests. The geography of Vietnam, in the shadow of its much larger neighbor, reinforces this tendency.

Future conflict over the South China Sea is a definite possibility, especially considering that four of the five potential flash points in the sea involve disputes between China and Vietnam.[21] This is not to argue that conflict is likely in the South China Sea, but that if the disputes were to become more acute, resulting, for example, from Vietnamese occupation of additional features in the Spratlys or initiation of petroleum exploration within Chinese-claimed zones, conflict may well ensue. Increasing Chinese naval presence and assertiveness in the South China Sea could also place Vietnam in a kowtow position by forcing it to abandon some of its sea claims in the face of Chinese power. Depending on the circumstances, Vietnam may either fight to support its claims or, more likely, as was done in the case of the Chinese oil rig off its coast in 1997, protest to its ASEAN neighbors to bring diplomatic pressure on Beijing, a type of action favoring the "due respect" scenario.

Vietnam's present ideological affinity with China could continue through this and the coming decade. The leadership of both countries may continue to justify their power by political ideology and to maintain the leading role of the Communist Party in their political systems. The attraction of a common ideology has already spawned the beginnings of a tributary relationship for Vietnam. Facing an uncertain future, with slowing economic development, environmental degradation, and social dislocation, Hanoi may cling to the hope that its future peace and prosperity are best assured by following the Chinese path. The premise of following that path is that modernization depends on stability, stability on strong central leadership, and strong central leadership on an ideology that justifies party control. Although the political and economic performance of both governments increasingly overshadows ideology as justification for continued rule, their common ideology remains, as shown in chapter 6, a strong factor unifying the leadership of both countries.

Closely linked to ideology, regime maintenance is at the heart of both Chinese and Vietnamese governmental concerns. As justification for continued party rule, the luster of revolutionary victories is wearing thin in both countries, so much so that their governments may be deceiving both themselves and their people about what really counts for regime maintenance—economic and political performance. To maintain political power, the leadership in Vietnam may continue to extol the "great achievements" of the People's Republic of China in the hope of convincing themselves and their people that Vietnam too can one day become a modern prosperous country like China. The purpose of an alliance or a kowtow relationship in this context would be to hold the Chinese model high in Vietnam and to justify continued party rule by emulating the policies of Beijing.

Economic benefit has both a short- and long-term dimension. While the current debate among Vietnamese leaders over the future direction of the economy appears to favor the Chinese model, including greater Chinese investment in and trade with Vietnam, the realists in the debate have better evidence that the long-term development of

Vietnam is best assured by the "due respect" scenario. Having secured normal trade relations with the United States, and planning for admittance into the WTO, Vietnam expects its opportunities for expanded trade and investment to multiply many times. Continued recovery of its neighbors from the Asian financial crisis of the late 1990s would bring even greater pressure on Vietnam to follow their paths of modernization, especially with regard to economic interdependence, legal reforms, and infrastructure development. China does and can play a role in stimulating the economy of Vietnam, but this role pales in comparison to the actual and potential roles of ASEAN, the United States, and the rest of the global economy.

U.S. Interests and the Four Scenarios

Before addressing which scenario best favors U.S. interests in Asia, it is necessary first to define those interests in terms of China and Vietnam, because U.S. post–World War II policy in Asia has been, to a large extent, a history of U.S. efforts to pursue its interests with respect to these two countries. Post–World War II U.S. support for the Chinese Nationalists both on the mainland and then on Taiwan, and for France and then the Republic of Vietnam in Indochina, was largely driven by a desire to contain international Communism. The principal rationale for this goal was the need to thwart a perceived Sino-Soviet attempt to dominate Asia, and in the case of Vietnam, to halt the spread of "wars of national liberation" that appeared to threaten U.S. friends and allies in less-developed areas of the world. In both cases, the success of Communist leaders was seen as a threat to the U.S. interests of peace and stability in Asia. Another important rationale was that the regimes in Beijing and Hanoi were seen as suppressing democracy, or at least precluding the development of democracy in their countries. In view of the weakness of the democratic tradition at the national level in both countries, this latter goal eventually evolved in U.S. support for two other current U.S. interests—political pluralism and respect for human rights. A fourth set of U.S. interests, free trade and investment, had its roots in the nineteenth century, at the end of which the well-known U.S. open-door policy sought to ensure U.S. business access to China.

These four sets of U.S. interests, peace and stability in Asia, free trade and investment, political pluralism, and respect for human rights, continue as the long-term goals of U.S. foreign policy in Asia today. They are spelled out in U.S. national policy statements from the White House to the departments of state and defense. They were reiterated clearly in administration statements justifying normalization of relations with Vietnam, granting of permanent normal trade relations (PNTR) to China, and normal trade relations to Vietnam. The following statement justifying PNTR typifies these statements:

> The question before the Congress is not whether China's record on human rights is defensible (it is not). The question is whether passage of PNTR will make positive change in China more or less likely. We believe it will make positive change more likely. We base that belief not on a simple-minded faith that increased trade automatically engenders democracy or more respect for human rights. We base it on the conviction that increased engagement, openness to ideas, and movement to new market forces will promote economic freedom and strengthen reformers trying to move policy there in the right direction. . . . The agreement will also strengthen the rule of law in China—that indispensable building block of a healthy polity, economic confidence, and civil society.[22]

The significance of future Sino-Vietnamese relations to the United States, therefore, is best judged by the degree to which those relations support or do not support these four specific sets of U.S. interests, as illustrated in table 7-2.

Table 7-2: Which Scenarios Favor Each U.S. Interest in Asia?*

U.S. Interest → Scenario ↴	Peace & Stability	Free Trade & Investment	Respect for Human Rights	Political Pluralism
Conflict	−	−	0	0
Alliance	0	0	−	−
Tribute	0	0	−	−
Due Respect	0	+	+	+

* "+" indicates support for U.S. interests, "0" neutral or mixed support for them, and "−" opposition to them.

The conflict scenario is in direct contrast to the U.S. interest in peace and stability. There was a time, in 1979, when the United States appeared to favor the Chinese border war with Vietnam, in part as a way of curtailing perceived Vietnamese aggression, but the rationale for that attitude has long since dissipated.[23] On the contrary, Washington now appears concerned that China might assert exaggerated maritime claims in the region. If it does so in conflict with Vietnam, particularly in the Con Son Basin, there could be an adverse effect on international shipping, as the sea-lanes through that disputed area are the second busiest in the world.[24] International investment in both countries is also likely to decline during any period of instability.

It would appear that human rights and political pluralism would remain unaffected by Sino-Vietnamese conflict. There is no evidence of any change in these categories during the 1979 war and its aftermath. However, it appears that the continuing diversion of Vietnamese resources to military readiness on the China border during the 1980s contributed to the economic deprivation that forced Vietnamese leaders to institute the limited economic reforms known as *doi moi*. Moreover, it could be argued that Chinese curtailment of Vietnam's offshore oil supply, by limiting Hanoi's access to a non-labor-intensive source of huge revenue, would make the Vietnamese government more dependent on its people and therefore more likely to tolerate greater rights for its citizens. Because of the need for strong central rule during conflict, however, the effect on political pluralism would be limited.

The alliance scenario appears, on the surface, to support some U.S. interests. It favors peace and stability insofar as the two former enemies and current principal protagonists in South China Sea disputes are at peace. It also favors increased trade and investment between China and Vietnam and enhances the prospects for joint exploration and development of ocean resources in the South China Sea, especially in the Gulf of Tonkin and the Con Son Basin, where there are no other claimants.

In contrast, the alliance scenario poses certain risks to U.S. interests. Southeast Asian countries are already deeply concerned about Chinese influence in the region, and an alliance with a country formerly seen as hostile would likely increase that concern. A Chinese military presence in Vietnam, for example, could polarize the region, increase Southeast Asian arms purchases, raise Philippine and Malaysian concerns about their claims in the South China Sea, and raise the specter of Chinese naval intrusions into nearby seas. Insofar as it might support an "Asia for the Asians" theme, an alliance could also undermine the U.S. interest in free trade and investment.[25] In addition, the maritime claims of Brunei, the Philippines, and Malaysia might be impaired. With respect to political pluralism and respect for human rights, an alliance of both countries as presently governed would likely signify an effort to maintain their regimes in order to control society without regard to these interests.

Like the alliance scenario, the kowtow scenario appears on the surface to favor peace and stability. By not positing Vietnamese opposition to expanded Chinese influence over the foreign and domestic politics of Vietnam, however, this scenario removes a check on Chinese ability to exert similar influence throughout Southeast Asia. For example, removal of Vietnamese opposition to Chinese claims in the South China Sea would seriously weaken Philippine and Malaysian claims, as well as the ASEAN multilateral approach to conflict resolution. There is also a possibility that the people of Vietnam, as they have many times during their history, would strongly oppose a government that kowtows to China in order to maintain legitimacy.

The tribute scenario closely resembles the alliance scenario with respect to other interests as well. It would have mixed results for external economic relations, increasing Sino-Vietnamese trade and investment but retarding Vietnamese relations with the rest of the global economy, including the United States. It would limit the influence of the United States and curtail emulation of U.S. political pluralism (which was at least shown respect in the past, when Ho Chi Minh patterned his declaration of independence on that of the United States and named his new regime the *Democratic* Republic of Vietnam). It would likely also reverse Vietnam's recent tendency to move slowly away from the Chinese pattern of repressing freedom of speech, assembly, and religion. In summary, the kowtow position does not serve U.S. interests well.

While the last scenario, a "due respect" relationship between Vietnam and China, poses modest risks of China punishing Vietnam for its tilt toward the non-Communist world, these risks could be minimized by prudent Vietnamese actions, such as avoiding giving permanent anchorage to foreign vessels in Cam Ranh Bay. Vietnamese military-to-military cooperation with the United States would have to lag behind that of the United States with China, in much the same way as its normal trade relations with the United States lagged behind those of the United States with China.[26]

In addition, Vietnam would have to carefully weigh any petroleum exploration in Chinese-claimed areas of the South China Sea. Its primary economic stimulus in this scenario would not lay with significantly greater revenues from oil and gas but with increased trade with and investment by the dynamic economies of Europe, Asia, and North America. With domestic policies and programs that facilitate such trade and investment, and international programs that promote technology transfer and education, the energetic people of Vietnam would likely transform their economy to their benefit and that of the United States.

Under the conditions of this scenario, the emphasis on private enterprise would take on additional significance. It has been the experience of U.S. business that the exchange of goods and services does not take place without an exchange of ideas—on how to develop sources of raw materials, to transport and process those materials, to set up efficient production lines, to build physical and human infrastructure, to train and motivate workers, to integrate production and distribution systems in an efficient way, and to market products successfully. Such exchanges, from top business and political leaders down to the worker in the factory, office, or farm, are the ingredients of change, for they would not only enable Vietnam to attain greater prosperity, but would also lead to greater freedom on which that prosperity rests. Ultimately, they could lead to greater political pluralism, as conservatives in the current regime well recognize with their antireform agenda.

In conclusion, it is clear that the "due respect" scenario best supports U.S. interests in Asia. It has minor risks for peace and stability in Asia, but no more so than other scenarios. It also enhances the prospects for respect for human rights and supports U.S. economic and political interests greater than any other scenario. The outstanding issue for U.S. policymakers, then, is how to encourage Vietnam to move toward this scenario in its important relationship with China.

U.S. Policy

There is no question regarding the relative importance of China and Vietnam to the United States. The time is long since past when Vietnam had the overarching importance in U.S. policy that it did a generation ago. Today, China is at the top of U.S. policy concerns both globally and in Asia. Issues of nonproliferation of weapons of mass destruction, Chinese policy toward Korea, the relationship of Taiwan to the mainland, human rights, and trade and investment have come to dominate U.S. policy concerns, so much so that the key U.S. ally in the region, Japan, is often neglected or taken for granted. And if Japan was a victim of benign neglect in the late 1990s, small and unallied Vietnam is fast becoming the obscure and distant country it was in the American consciousness before it became the plug in the dike of containment of international Communism. Vietnam is simply not an important part of U.S. foreign policy in the twenty-first century.

Under these conditions, U.S. policy needs to address the Sino-Vietnamese relationship primarily as it affects China. U.S. policy, after all, is focused on China. The real issue is how much U.S. policy toward Vietnam's China relationship can affect China, if at all. Viewed from this perspective, Vietnam has a special importance in U.S. policy because of its relationship with China. That importance is highlighted in the "due respect" relationship, in which Vietnam supports U.S. interests by internal reforms and external relations that might influence China. While formulating a policy toward Vietnam that is not directed against legitimate Chinese interests, the United States may also stimulate change in Vietnam that results in emulation by China. The bottom line is that a Vietnam that succeeds in its developmental path could, as a result of policies identified with the "due respect" scenario, serve in some respects as a model for China, terminate a trend toward the tributary relationship, and avoid the problems that the conflict and alliance scenarios pose to U.S interests in Asia.

To promote the "due respect" relationship, U.S. policy needs to recognize and support, to the extent possible, the four factors identified in table 7-1 as favoring that scenario—national culture, national independence, stability in the South China Sea, and economic benefit.

At first glance, it would appear that the United States cannot do much to promote traditional popular Vietnamese culture, for culture by its nature is an internal matter. However, today's Vietnam is facing challenges of modernization that place considerable stress on its traditional values of strong family and village ties. A dramatic rise in drug use, prostitution, abortion, and abuse of women has taken place in the past decade. While the U.S. Department of State human rights report identifies some of these problems, it does little to provide solutions to them.[27] U.S. support for traditional Vietnamese cultural values might include:

- increased support for the rule of law, including respect for Vietnamese laws and restrictions against the import into Vietnam of pornographic materials
- participation in bilateral and multilateral donor initiatives that promote reforms to reduce the poverty underlying many societal problems
- continued promotion of free enterprise, with emphasis on its employment benefits
- further diplomatic support for freedom of religion as a way of reinforcing traditional values
- additional educational exchanges and support for U.S. teaching programs in Vietnam
- support for nongovernment organization efforts to assist the marginalized segments of society
- cooperation with Vietnamese authorities in their efforts to eliminate the illicit drug trade

U.S. policy should also appeal to Vietnamese culture in its calls for democracy. With the exception of sporadic attempts by the former South Vietnam, Vietnam does not have a history of democracy at the national level. Leading citizens, however, traditionally picked their local leaders and village chiefs, and village notables routinely expressed their views on community projects. As education and greater societal awareness continue to develop in modern Vietnam, this traditional cultural proclivity to participate in local decisions is increasingly being felt at higher levels. Thus district and provincial councils, and to a lesser degree the National Assembly, are beginning to exert a modicum of political influence.

U.S. policy cannot and should not try to control or take credit for this indigenous "peaceful evolution." Nebulous calls for democracy raise fears among controlling elements of the leadership, who view "peaceful evolution" as foreign inspired and directed. On the contrary, U.S appeals for reform in Vietnam should focus on indigenous

Vietnamese goals such as empowering the people. In private, U.S. diplomats should take the position that democratic reforms in Vietnam are consistent with the traditional aspirations of the Vietnamese people, such as a moral code of conduct with emphasis on human rights exemplified in the Hong Duc Code of the fifteenth century. They should offer specific advice and assistance on building democratic institutions, showing recognition that the rule of law will take time and emphasizing checks and balances as a framework for true reform. As a symbolic bottom line, they might encourage Hanoi to put the word "democratic" back into the title of the nation.[28]

U.S. support for the independence of Vietnam is limited in two ways. First, it cannot become involved in supporting expatriates planning or executing violent actions against the regime. This does not mean that the United States should support the regime in Hanoi against domestic unrest, but that it should not give justification for the regime to link that unrest to outside-inspired "hostile forces." The U.S. role in such circumstances is to speak out on behalf of the rights of all peoples to determine their own destiny. Second, the United States cannot and should not become engaged in direct military action to support Vietnam against China, as China is the only nation with both the means and a potential motive to attack that country. Encouragement of Vietnam to confront China militarily could lead to Vietnamese requests for U.S. military assistance, but such assistance is unlikely to have the support of the people of the United States. Despite these limitations, the United States has followed policies that demonstrate support for a more independent Vietnam. These include:

- support for Vietnam's admission to ASEAN in 1995
- normalization of relations in 1995, and
- the granting of normal trade relations in 2001

Additional steps are possible. First, the United States should encourage Vietnam to embrace the information revolution more fully. Vietnam launched an information technology program at the end of 1997, but computers in the global network are still limited to some 60,000 students. Hanoi plans to expand student access, but the overwhelming majority of Vietnamese citizens do not own a computer and cannot afford web access.[29] Further information access could, as it has in the

United States, provide significant educational and economic benefits. These, in turn, provide the people the means to move beyond the student-teacher relationship that is now reasserting itself in Vietnam's relations with China.

Second, the United States should publicly recognize and reward Vietnam when it adheres to international principles. Unlike China, Vietnam is not exporting weapons of mass destruction or threatening its neighbors. It seeks to avoid entangling alliances with major powers and is moving, albeit slowly, toward more humane internal policies. Finally, the United States should treat Vietnam on its own merits, and not as a pawn in its relationship with China. The United States should not lag in its economic and political engagement with Vietnam out of deference to China, but engage it as the fully independent state that it has become.[30]

The third factor favoring the "due respect" scenario is peace and stability in the South China Sea. U.S. policy currently focuses on peace and stability as it pertains to freedom of navigation, a commitment to the Philippines under the Mutual Defense Treaty, and support for ASEAN confidence-building measures. Freedom of navigation is not a major issue in most of the South China Sea, because the heavily trafficked international sea-lanes do not pass through the disputed waters of the Spratlys, Paracels, or the Tonkin Gulf. They do pass through disputed waters in the Con Son Basin, but even a conflict in that zone would require only that the ships take alternate routes.[31] Likewise, the U.S. defense treaty with the Philippines applies primarily to defense of the metropolitan territory of the Philippines, and not Philippine-claimed areas in the Spratlys, on which the United States takes no position regarding the merits of the claims by China, Vietnam, the Philippines, Malaysia, and Taiwan. The only forward-leaning aspect of U.S. policy is support for ASEAN efforts to establish confidence-building measures, but even there the United States plays a secondary role.[32]

Although U.S. policy has thus far kept the United States from becoming embroiled in conflict in the South China Sea, that policy has been criticized for being too passive. It calls for nonviolence and freedom of navigation, but it takes no position on competing claims. Additional U.S. measures that may enhance the prospects for peace and stability in the South China Sea include the following:

- support overhead satellite reconnaissance to monitor military activity[33]
- conduct periodic naval maneuvers in the area, including freedom of navigation operations in the Spratlys
- participate in an oil and gas survey of the Spratlys with the intention of demonstrating that existing petroleum resources are not worth fighting over
- support international judicial and investigative tribunals that can provide options for eventual distribution of resources within the South China Sea
- call for multilateral solutions involving all claimants to enhance the prospects for peaceful resolution of outstanding disputes

The final factor favoring the "due respect" scenario, economic benefit, is more clearly subject to influence by U.S. policy. Hanoi initiated limited private enterprise in the late 1980s to save the country from economic crisis, but as it begins the twenty-first century, Hanoi continues to favor corrupt or ill-managed state-owned enterprises that it can better control. The result is that Vietnam has not been able to realize its potential of becoming an Asian economic "tiger." Instead of relying on the considerable entrepreneurial skills of its people, it relies on a heavy dose of foreign aid along with profits from offshore oil and gas. Under these circumstances, U.S. policy should:

- support nongovernmental organization assistance to Vietnam, but not become part of the massive aid program on which Vietnam has become accustomed to rely for basic economic needs
- point out that the Chinese economy, insofar as it has had limited success, has been successful primarily because of free enterprise reforms
- continue to insist, both in negotiations leading to its entry into the WTO and in considering permanent normal trade relations, that Vietnam open its economy to market forces
- support, through education and exchanges of political and economic leaders, the development of a legal infrastructure that facilitates orderly business and commerce

CHAPTER 8

Conclusion

Amerian policy in East Asia has, for generations, been designed to
prevent the domination of the region by a single power. China
today is far from having the capability to dominate Asia, but it does
give evidence of intent to control the foreign and security policies of
Vietnam—to lock it into a subservient relationship characteristic of
the tributary status Vietnam experienced for over a thousand years.
This would appear to be of no account to the United States. But closer
examination points to the fact that an independent Vietnam, free to
choose its own domestic and international agenda, is far more attuned
to U.S. interests in Asia than is a Vietnam subservient to or in alliance
with Beijing. U.S. policy can influence Vietnam in the direction of a
"due respect" scenario, in which opportunities abound for Vietnam to
become not a domino in some cold war analogy, but a dynamo in the
modern interdependent Asian and global economy.

By contributing to a Vietnam that excels in political, economic,
and social development, the United States may cause China to reassess
its own path of modernization out of sheer embarrassment that its
smaller neighbor was beginning to surpass it in its modernization efforts.
Such a development is a long way from realization under the present
policies of Hanoi, but might ultimately prevail with a Vietnamese
reorientation away from China and toward the dynamic political and
economic regimes of the global marketplace.

Such reorientation will require courage on the part of the leadership in Hanoi. Vietnam remains, after all its wars and struggles for
independence, in the shadow of the dragon. Geography does not change,
and China will always loom large in Vietnamese thinking. Vietnam's

political system, economic performance, national security, and technological progress are all greatly influenced by China. While current
Chinese and Vietnamese officials like to explain this in terms of connecting rivers and mountains, Vietnamese and other Southeast Asian leaders
are particularly apprehensive about what they perceive as "the rise of
China" in recent years. They see a new and not necessarily benign
power flexing its muscles in areas of trade, maritime claims, and foreign
policy. Their tendency is to reach accommodation with China.

For Vietnam this is nothing new. The fact is that for over 2,000
years Vietnam has worried about absorption by its northern neighbor.
In so doing, it goes through a cycle that has repeated itself numerous
times throughout history. The cycle begins with Chinese pressure on
Vietnam to accommodate to its expanding power and needs. Vietnam
typically responds by accommodation, Sinicization, and acceptance of
the appointment of a mandarin class responsive to Chinese demands.
The mandarin class, often Chinese in origin, levies taxes, demands
corvée labor, and extorts goods and services until the oppression becomes
popularly perceived as tyranny. A revolt breaks out in which the rebellious army fights a mandarin faction loyal to the Chinese emperor. A
Chinese army is sent to support the loyal faction, but the Vietnamese
army eventually defeats it. Having won the struggle, the new leaders
of Vietnam hasten to renew tribute to the Chinese emperor, both to
conciliate him and to gain his support for their new government. A
period of stability ensues, but eventually the new government becomes
too dependent on the court in Beijing. Its power base is no longer the
people of Vietnam but the goodwill of the Chinese court. Corruption
increases. Chinese pressure is renewed, mandarins who resist are replaced, popular discontent again arises, and the vicious cycle repeats
itself.

The Vietnam of today is no less susceptible to this cycle than the
Vietnam of history. Having inflicted heavy casualties on the invading
People's Liberation Army in 1979, and having resisted 10 years of
pressure along the border, Vietnam has again hastened to pay homage
to its great northern neighbor. Both the Vietnamese government and
party court the Chinese in every way, lavishly praising the Chinese
system of governance, repeatedly and profoundly thanking Beijing for
its economic assistance, and largely deferring to China in the settlement
of the Tonkin Gulf dispute.

Yet there are voices in Vietnam today that call for a different path. While recognizing the need to pay due respect to China, they also recognize that Vietnam today has a unique opportunity to break from excessive dependence on China by pursuing the path of independence for which Vietnam has fought throughout its history. They seek to retain, in the face of Chinese counterclaims, Vietnamese-held features in the Spratly Islands and the Con Son Basin. They see in the bilateral trade agreement with the United States an opportunity to dramatically increase Vietnamese exports. They look to alternative political and economic structures as models for development, and seek a multidirectional foreign policy with close ties to the Association of Southeast Asian Nations, Japan, the Republic of Korea, Taiwan, Europe, and the United States.

Striking a balance between due respect for China and emulation of and close relations with these areas of the world will not be an easy task for Hanoi. The cultural and political "pull" of Vietnam is toward China; despite the demise of colonialism and its national unification, its political leadership continues to live in the shadow of the larger dragon to the north. Nevertheless, Vietnam also has a history of looking outward. Its centuries-old "push" to the south was characteristic of a people looking to fulfill a new and independent destiny. Its adaptation of Western learning, its solicitation of external assistance in times of crisis, and its ability to attract international donors in time of peace all demonstrate an outward-looking orientation. Likewise, recent calls for a multidirectional foreign policy, opening to the international community, and assertion of rights to offshore resources are all modern reflections of a deeply rooted Vietnamese desire for independence.

Under these circumstances, the United States has the opportunity to extend to Vietnam the hand of friendship and assistance. Support for the rule of law, peace, and stability in the South China Sea; political and economic development; free enterprise; and human rights are all part of U.S. policy toward Vietnam. The key to achieving success toward these ends is not to berate Vietnam for lack of progress toward these goals, but to emphasize that they serve Vietnamese self-interest, including the ever-present desire to cut a path that is independent of the powerful influence of its northern neighbor.

While some past U.S. policies toward Vietnam were flawed, the best elements of those policies called for a then South Vietnam to be free and independent from Soviet and Chinese domination. The premise of that domination may be debated, but the objective of a free and independent Vietnam remains today, as it did a generation ago, in the U.S. interest. By promoting policies that are attuned to traditional Vietnamese culture, support Vietnamese independence, maintain stability in the South China Sea, and highlight the benefits of the free enterprise system within a more democratic framework, the United States can help Vietnam toward a truly free and independent status. In so doing, the United States can honor the efforts of the past, both Vietnamese and American, and help build a better life for future generations of both countries.

NOTES

Chapter 1: Introduction

1. Since the People's Army of Vietnam (PAVN) withdrew from Cambodia, Hanoi has reduced the size of its military forces by more than half, with the remaining forces ill-equipped with modern weapons and inexperienced in combat. Conversely, China's People's Liberation Army has an ongoing modernization program that includes air and naval forces far superior to those of Vietnam, especially with respect to capabilities in any possible future conflict in the South China Sea.

Chapter 2: China, Vietnam, and U.S. Policy in Perspective

1. For Hamburger Hill, see Lieutenant General E. M. Flanagan, *The Rakkasans: The Combat History of the 187th Airborne Infantry* (Novato, Calif.: Presidio Press, 1997). The Khe Sanh figure includes over 400 Americans killed in and around Khe Sanh after the siege was supposedly lifted. See Peter Brush, "The Withdrawl from Khe Sanh," *Vietnam* (August 1997).

2. At one point, former U.S. secretary of state Henry Kissinger reportedly stated that 500,000 U.S. soldiers have settled the importance of Vietnam.

3. Joseph Stilwell, *The Stilwell Papers* (Da Capo Press, reprint, 1991) New York: Sloane Associates, 1948; and Barbara Tuchman, *Stilwell and the American Experience in China, 1911–1945* (New York: Macmillan Co., 1970).

4. Former South Vietnamese premier Nguyen Cao Ky, in remarks at West Point, New York, 1972.

5. U.S. Department of Commerce, Bureau of the Census, "U.S. Trade Balance with China," *International Trade Statistics* (Washington, D.C.: U.S. Department of Commerce, 2000).

6. Robert Burns, "Pentagon to Look into Asian Military," Associated Press, 18 December 2000.

7. Franklin D. Roosevelt, "Remarks on French Possessions," Department of State, *Foreign Relations of the United States* (Washington, D.C.: U.S. Government Printing Office, 1968), 514; Conversations with Kenneth Landon, U.S. consul in Hanoi in 1946.

8. In April 1950 the Democratic Republic of Vietnam described itself as a "People's Democracy" and announced support for the Communist liberation movement in Cambodia. See Allan W. Cameron, ed., *Vietnam Crisis—A Documentary History, Volume 1: 1940–1956* (Ithaca, N.Y.: Cornell University Press, 1971).

9. In the cold war at that time, this was considered a serious issue. The U.S. intelligence community estimated that there were 175 Soviet divisions in Eastern Europe, compared to 12 NATO divisions. In April 1950 the U.S. Joint Chiefs of Staff recommended, and the president approved the following month, $10 million in military assistance

for French Indochina. The Department of Defense, *The Pentagon Papers, U.S.-Vietnam Relations, 1945–1967* (Washington, D.C.: U.S. Government Printing Office, 1971), vol 2, 17; Dwight D. Eisenhower, "Report to NATO Planning Committee," 10 October 1951, cited in Louis J. Halle, *The Cold War as History* (New York: Harper Perennial, 1991), 184–86.

10. Author discussions with U.S. servicemen, Ft. Campbell, Kentucky, 1962, and Ft. Bragg, North Carolina, 1965. For details on aid to France, see Defense Department, *Pentagon Papers,* vol. 1, 1–10 and 26–35; Dean Acheson, *Present at the Creation* (New York: W. W. Norton and Co, 1969), 429 and 856–63.

11. "JCS Memorandum for the Secretary of Defense," 26 May 1954, in Defense Department, *Pentagon Papers,* vol. 9, 487.

12. Ibid., vol. 4, 60.

13. U.S. aid dropped from $393 million in 1957 to $253 million in 1960, Eisenhower's last year in office. Ibid., vol. 4, 37.

14. The term Viet Minh is an abbreviation of *Vietnam Doc Lap Dong Minh Hoi,* or Vietnam Independence League, the Communist-dominated nationalist front that led the struggle against the French from 1946 to 1954. Viet Cong, or Vietnamese Communist, is the American term for the nationalist front's Southern Vietnamese opponents during the Vietnam War.

15. These views are reiterated in Acheson, *Present at the Creation.*

16. John F. Kennedy, *America's Stake in Vietnam* (New York: American Friends of Vietnam, 1956), 10.

17. In the fall of 1963, Kennedy announced his intention to cut the number of U.S. military advisers by 1,000, partly in response to Diem's raids on Buddhist pagodas. During an interview with Walter Cronkite on 2 September 1963, he stated: "In the final analysis it is their war. They are the ones who have to win or lose it. We can help them, we can give them equipment, we can send our men out there as advisers, but they must win it—the people of Vietnam alone against the Communists." Four days later, at a National Security Council meeting, he asked his advisers: "Have we not overestimated the U.S role in Vietnam?" See Roger Hilsman, *To Move a Nation* (Garden City, N.Y.: Doubleday and Co., 1967), 501; CBS News Interview with President Kennedy, 2 September 1963.

18. Statement by President Lyndon B. Johnson, 2 June 1964, Department of State, *U.S. Policy in Background Information Relating to Southeast Asia and Vietnam* (Washington, D.C.: U.S. Government Printing Office, July 1967), 128–29.

19. Lyndon B. Johnson, "Vietnam: The Struggle to Be Free," address at the Freedom House Dinner in New York, 23 February 1966, in *Vantage Point: Perspectives of the Presidency, 1963–1969* (New York: Holt, Rinehart, and Winston, 1971), 390.

20. General William Westmoreland reportedly asked for 206,000 additional soldiers, of which the president approved only 13,500, bringing total authorized U.S troop strength in Vietnam to 549,500, the high-water mark of U.S. military presence in Vietnam. Neil Sheehan and Hedrick Smith, *New York Times,* 10 March 1968; "The President's Address to the Nation," 31 March 1968.

21. For a detailed analysis of these and other events surrounding the policy shift, see Henry J. Kenny, "The Changing Importance of Vietnam in United States Policy: 1949–1969" (Ph.D. Dissertation, American University, 1974).

22. Richard M. Nixon, "The Pursuit of Peace," 3 November 1969 (Washington, D.C.: Department of State Publication 8502, November 1969), 8.

23. The author was the professional staff member with the delegation. When Vice Foreign Minister Phan Hien read the letter to the delegation in December 1975, it was not stated as a demand, but was presented with a clear expectation that the United States would honor its "commitment" to Vietnam. The letter came as a complete surprise to the delegation, especially as members had asked Kissinger, just before visiting Vietnam, if there were any secret deals with Hanoi. The secretary had replied that "you have been given all the information." After the delegation returned to Washington, Kissinger refused to meet with it, and it then met with Deputy Secretary of State Philip Habib. Habib swore he did not know of the existence of the letter.

24. Richard Holbrooke, then assistant secretary of state for East Asia and Pacific Affairs, was a key proponent of the normalization talks, which were held in Paris.

25. Vietnam eventually returned the remains of over 300 U.S. servicemen. Many of the remains given to the United States as possible MIAs turned out to be Vietnamese rather than Americans.

26. China, of course, played a significant role in Hanoi's decision to withdraw from Cambodia. Every time the People's Army of Vietnam launched a major campaign against the Khmer Rouge, China's People's Liberation Army would respond, mostly with heavy artillery barrages along the border, and occasionally with raids just inside the border. China reduced the level and scope of these activities during the late 1980s as Hanoi took steps to reduce its military presence in Cambodia.

27. Other war-related issues declined in importance. These included Amerasian children and reeducation camp prisoners. Vietnam had inhumanely treated both groups, but by 1995, most Amerasians had left the country and most reeducation camp prisoners had been released. By the mid-1990s, the dramatic exodus of large numbers of boat people had also come to an end, as both the Orderly Departure Program and the designation of fewer Vietnamese as political refugees resulted in far fewer departures by sea.

28. President Nixon met with Premier Nguyen Van Thieu. En route Nixon articulated his Guam Doctrine in which he signaled his intent to turn the bulk of the fighting in Vietnam over to the Vietnamese.

29. Remarks by Charlene Barshefsky, United States trade representative, on the U.S.-Vietnam Bilateral Trade Agreement, before hearing of the House International Relations Committee, 19 September 2000.

30. President Bill Clinton, "Remarks by the President on the Announcement of Vietnam Bilateral Trade Agreement," Office of the Press Secretary, the White House, 13 July 2000.

31. President Bill Clinton, address at the Vietnam National University, Hanoi, 17 November 2000, as reported by the White House.

32. Author's notes on a meeting between Premier Pham Van Dong and members of the House Select Committee on Missing Persons in Southeast Asia. Committee members visited Hanoi in December 1975 to initiate the postwar effort to account for missing Americans.

33. Ibid.

34. Nayan Chanda, "Blowing Hot and Cold," *Far East Economic Review,* 30 November 2000, 22–24. Hereafter *FEER.*

Chapter 3: The Historical Legacy

1. These words adorned public buildings in Hanoi for years after the North defeated the South. Most Vietnamese, while agreeing with the expression, are concerned that the "freedom" part of the expression has made but meager progress in recent years.

2. Dong Xuan Hoa, "The Fairy's Tale," *Tap Chi cua Hang Khong Quoc Gia Vietnam* (January/February, 1999): 34–38, presents a romantic view of this story, in which Loc Long Quan saved the life of a crane that was then transformed into the princess Au Co. See also Oscar Chapuis, *A History of Vietnam from Hong Bang to Tu Duc* (London: Greenwood Press, 1995), 10–11.

3. D. G. E. Hall, *A History of Southeast Asia,* 4th ed. (New York: St. Martin's Press, 1981), 211–12; Chapuis, *A History of Vietnam,* 13–15.

4. Joseph Buttinger, *Vietnam: A Political History* (New York: Praeger, 1968), 20–23; Hall, *A History of Southeast Asia,* 212.

5. Spencer C. Tucker, *Vietnam* (Lexington: The University of Kentucky Press, 1999), 5–7.

6. Chapuis, *A History of Vietnam,* 3, 25, 27; Hall, *A History of Southeast Asia,* 212. The Chinese renamed the kingdom Chiao-Chou, of which Ghiao-Chih consisted of the present Red River valley and surrounding areas.

7. Chapuis, *A History of Vietnam,* 27–28; Buttinger, *Vietnam,* 8–10.

8. Hall, *A History of Southeast Asia,* 212–13.

9. Tucker, *Vietnam,* 6–7, gives a concise description the conditions for Vietnamese revolt at this time.

10. Chapuis, *A History of Vietnam,* 33–34.

11. Pham Van Vinh, *Vietnam: A Comprehensive History* (Solana Beach, Calif.: PM Enterprises, 1992), 66.

12. Chapuis, *A History of Vietnam,* 33–34.

13. King C. Chen, *China's War with Vietnam, 1979: Issues, Decisions, and Implications* (Stanford, Calif.: Hoover Institution Press, 1987), 100–101.

14. For a detailed description of this and other periods of Chinese rule, see Keith W. Taylor, *The Birth of Vietnam* (Berkeley: University of California Press, 1983). Taylor divides Chinese rule into six phases and demonstrates how Vietnam developed and reinforced its national identity in the face of sometime harsh Chinese rule, particularly under the T'ang.

15. Buttinger, *Vietnam,* 35–36.

16. Hall, *A History of Southeast Asia,* 35.

17. In subsequent squabbles between Champa and Annam, the Chinese told the squabbling sides to govern their hereditary realms and pay tribute. Ibid., 35–36, 219.

18. Ibid., 203.

19. Chapuis, *A History of Vietnam,* 33.

20. The appeal for Chinese help has been described in Vietnamese literature as "bringing home the snake to have your chickens killed." Pham Van Vinh, *A Comprehensive History,* 69.

21. Its capital was at Co La a dozen miles from Hanoi, where the remains of a citadel testify to its ancient importance. Hall, *A History of Southeast Asia,* 939; Author's discussions with officials of the Museum of History, Hanoi, 1993.

22. Pham Van Vinh, *A Comprehensive History,* 72.

23. Both Ly Thuong Kiet and Ton Dan won big victories over China. The attacks were to prevent the Chinese from retaliating against Ly Nhan Tong's policy of promoting Vietnamese business interests at the expense of the Chinese. Ibid., 76; Chapuis, *A History of Vietnam*, 73–77.

24. This was not enough for the Great Khan, whose ambassador scolded Tran Thanh Tong's successor, Tran Nhan Tong, for assuming the throne without the Chinese emperor's approval. Chapuis, *A History of Vietnam*, 81–83.

25. Ibid.; Tucker, *Vietnam*, 11.

26. Chapuis, *A History of Vietnam*, 79–85. Although Tran Hung Dao was the greatest hero to rise to and meet the invasion, there were many others. The Vietnamese general Tran Binh Trong, for example, when offered by China the position of administrator of northern Annam, replied, "I prefer to be a demon in the South than a king in the North." Conversely, there were a number of collaborators, often referred to as *Viet gian*, or traitors.

27. Chinese Buddhism is of the Mahayana, or "greater vehicle," type, intended to bring people the enlightenment through Buddhist thought and way of life. Mahayana Buddhists, including those in north and central Vietnam, refer to the variety of Buddhism in Southeast Asia as the Hinayana, or "lesser vehicle." Many Southeast Asians, including those in the southern regions of modern Vietnam, resent this term and refer to themselves as Theravada Buddhists, practicing a purer form of the teachings of Saddartha Gautama, the founder of Buddhism.

28. Hall, *A History of Southeast Asia*, 202; Pham Van Vinh, *A Comprehensive History*, 74–75.

29. Vinh, *A Comprehensive History*. The oldest university in Vietnam, the Van Mieu in Hanoi, consisted of rigorous study of the Chinese classics and Confucian thought.

30. When Yün-nan threatened to become Islamic, the Chinese sent an army to crush the movement. The Ming demanded that the Vietnamese supply the Chinese army and also pay additional tribute in the form of rice and wood. Chapuis, *A History of Vietnam*, 93.

31. Ibid., 87 and 97–98; Buttinger, *Vietnam*, 44–45.

32. Joseph Buttinger, *A Dragon Defiant: A Short History of Vietnam* (New York: Praeger, 1972), 45.

33. William J. Duiker, *Vietnam: Nation in Revolution* (Boulder, Colo.: Westview Press, 1983), 19; Chapuis, *A History of Vietnam*, 102–107. A myth attending the story of Le Loi parallels that of Sir Lancelot of King Arthur's court. A dragon emerged from a lake in present-day Hanoi and presented Le Loi a sword to drive out the Chinese. After doing so with the help of the sword, Le Loi returned the sword to the lake, known today as Ho Hoan Kiem, or Lake of the Return of the Sword.

34. Hall, *A History of Southeast Asia*, 208–209 and 215–16.

35. Ibid., 210; Chapuis, *A History of Vietnam*, 133.

36. Chapuis, *A History of Vietnam*, 113–14.

37. One of the reasons for the Trinh success was the decline of the Ming dynasty in China. A year after the Trinh captured Hanoi, the great Japanese warlord Hideoshi successfully attacked Korea. The Ming forces were on the defensive everywhere, and by 1644 were replaced by the Ch'ing dynasty. See John F. Cady, *Southeast Asia: Its Historical Development* (New York: McGraw-Hill, 1964), 264; Hall, *A History of Southeast Asia*, 219.

38. Hall, *A History of Southeast Asia,* 220; Chapuis, *A History of Vietnam,* 161; and Cady, *Southeast Asia,* 443. Some 3,000 of these settled at My Tho and Bien Hoa in southern Vietnam.

39. Hall, *A History of Southeast Asia,* 443.

40. Chapuis, *A History of Vietnam,* 124.

41. Hall, *A History of Southeast Asia,* 438–41. Overseas Chinese were some of the most ambitious in developing the new lands.

42. Although the Trinh did receive some Dutch support, the Dutch pulled out after the Nguyen sank one of their ships and nearly captured two others. The Portuguese provided more substantial support to the Nguyen, including a cannon factory and a large number of ships.

43. It is a coincidence of history that this Vietnamese revolution occurred at the very time the American founding fathers were declaring that whenever any form of government becomes destructive of life, liberty, and the pursuit of happiness, "it is the right of the people to alter or to abolish it." Action of the Second Continental Congress, *The Declaration of Independence,* 4 July 1776. Some scholars attribute the severe conditions and lack of economic development at this time as attributable to the persistence of Confucian culture. See Duiker, *Vietnam,* 22.

44. Duiker, *Vietnam,* 21–24; Vinh, *A Comprehensive History,* 95–97.

45. Chapuis, *A History of Vietnam,* 137–38 and 159–69.

46. Duiker, *Vietnam,* 21–24.

47. The tribute was modest: elephant tusks, rhinoceros horns, cinnamon, some gold, silver, and silk. But the kowtow was large. When a Chinese delegation arrived in Hanoi, Gia Long had laid a red carpet from the Red River landing point to the capital. Chapuis, *A History of Vietnam,* 182.

48. Hall, *A History of Southeast Asia,* 454.

49. The four classes were *si* (landlord scholars); *nong* (farmers); *cong* (artisans); and, the lowest, *thuong* (merchants).

50. Chapuis, *A History of Vietnam,* 181–83.

51. For an excellent description of both court and popular Vietnamese adoption of Chinese ways during the nineteenth century, see Alexander B. Woodside, *Vietnam and the Chinese Model: A Comparative Study of Vietnamese and Chinese Government in the First Half of the Nineteenth Century* (Cambridge, Mass.: Harvard University Press, 1988). For a detailed analysis of the Vietnamese at that time and through the mid-twentieth century, see Oscar Chapuis, *The Last Emperors of Vietnam: From Tu Duc to Bao Dai* (Westwood, Conn.: Greenwood Press, 2000).

52. Hall, *A History of Southeast Asia,* 685–88.

53. Ibid., 686; Vinh, *A Comprehensive History,* 115–20; Cady, *Southeast Asia,* 421–23. Troops from southern China once again attacked the French in 1885, but the French defeated them at Son Tay. The French labeled the Chinese troops "black flag pirates."

54. See chapter 4 for details.

55. Hall, *A History of Southeast Asia,* 696–705; and Buttinger, *Vietnam,* 96–97.

56. Hall, *A History of Southeast Asia,* 802; and Buttinger, *Vietnam,* 121–22 and 142–43. See also William Duiker, *Ho Chi Minh* (New York: Hyperion, 2000) for an excellent description of Chau's role in Vietnam's revolutionary movement and his relationship with Ho Chi Minh.

57. Hall, *A History of Southeast Asia,* 803–806.

58. Duiker, *Vietnam.* Ho Chi Minh was said to have betrayed his former teacher, Phan Boi Chau, by inviting him to a house in Shanghai, where he told the French they could capture Chau. Ho was also said to have delivered pictures of cadets trained at Whampoa, but not loyal to his organization, to the French. Vinh, *A Comprehensive History,* 129–30. See William J. Duiker, *China and Vietnam: The Roots of Conflict,* Indochina research monograph 1 (Berkeley, Calif.: Institute of East Asian Studies, University of California, 1986). The story of American support for Ho Chi Minh's guerrillas is told in Ellen Hammer, *The Struggle for Indochina* (Stanford, Calif.: Stanford University Press, 1954), and by King C. Chen, *Vietnam and China, 1938–1954* (Princeton, N.J.: Princeton University Press, 1969), 90–98.

59. Bernard Fall, *The Two Vietnams: A Political and Military Analysis* (New York: Praeger Pubs., 1963), 66–71. Ho also claimed he had U.S. support because of his association with the Office of Strategic Services and the U.S. South China Command.

60. Vinh, *A Comprehensive History,* 217–25. The Chinese Nationalist Government agreed to withdraw its occupation troops from Vietnam only after France had ceded its special rights in China.

61. Federal Research Division, Library of Congress, *Vietnam: A Country Study* (Washington, D.C.: U.S. Government Printing Office, 1987), 51–58.

62. Vinh, *A Comprehensive History,* 293. Vietnamese officials in Hanoi expressed a similar theme to the author in 1999. It is clear, however, that at this time both China and Russia were advancing their "peaceful coexistence" line, so that Vietnam had little room to maneuver between the two. In addition, China may have been concerned about U.S. intervention, as the U.S. position was "to give its expressed or implied approval to any cease-fire, armistice, or other settlement which would have the effect of subverting the existing lawful governments of the aforementioned (Indochinese) states." Presidential Instructions to the U.S. Delegation, 12 May 1954, *Pentagon Papers,* vol. 9 (Washington, D.C.: U.S. Government Printing Office, 1973), 457–59.

63. Vinh, *A Comprehensive History,* 355–56; Chen, *Vietnam and China,* 331–45.

64. Fall, *The Two Vietnams,* 450.

65. This attitude carried over to the period of colonial rule, when the Vietnamese revolutionaries viewed the imperial court as a puppet of the French.

66. Among the many similarities of Vietnamese history to the American revolutionary period was the critical attack on the Chinese outpost at Son Nam while its defenders were celebrating the New Year (Tet) festival, an action closely paralleling George Washington's attack on the Hessians at Trenton over the Christmas holidays in 1776. Nguyen Hue's strategy was to attack south to eliminate his opponent Nguyen Anh and then strike north to defeat the Chinese. In 1978 Hanoi decided to repeat this strategy, striking first to eliminate a threat from Cambodia and then "striking north" to face an expected Chinese border attack. A Vietnamese general described this strategy to the author in 1999 as *dang nam ra bac* (strike the south and then confront the north).

67. Ho Chi Minh proclaimed the Democratic Republic of Vietnam (DRV) in 1946. After defeating South Vietnam, Hanoi renamed the country the Socialist Republic of Vietnam. While the title of the Democratic Republic of Vietnam was a misnomer, it inspired at least some Vietnamese as an ideal. Although the United States had no intention of "invading" Vietnam, DRV leaders portrayed the U.S. intervention in that manner.

68. "Between 1803 and 1853, the Nguyen rulers sent 14 missions to Beijing. Their government structure became so Sinicized that their leaders were called sons of heaven and . . . they called their court the Trung Quoc (Middle Kingdom), as China did." Steven J. Hood, *Dragons Entangled: Indochina and the China-Vietnam War* (New York: M. E. Sharpe, 1992), 12.

Chapter 4: Land Border and South China Sea Disputes

1. Pao-min Chang, *The Sino-Vietnamese Territorial Dispute* (Washington, D.C.: Center for Strategic Studies, 1986), 12.
2. Statement by an interviewee in author's interview with high-ranking officers of the People's Army of Vietnam in Hanoi, 1999. The PAVN officers stated that the USSR helped instigate the Korean War to drive a deep wedge between the United States and China.
3. Ibid.; Chang, *The Sino-Vietnamese Territorial Dispute.*
4. Statement by interviewee during author's interview with former senior Vietnamese diplomats, Hanoi, 1999.
5. Chang, *The Sino-Vietnamese Territorial Dispute,* in chapters 2–4, describes the land and sea border disputes in detail. Vietnamese officials spoke disparagingly about Chinese policy in several meetings with the author from 1975 to 1984.
6. Statement made by a foreign ministry official to author in Hanoi, October 1993.
7. Henry J. Kenny, "Vietnamese Perceptions of the 1979 War with China," in *PLA Warfighting: Essays in the Modern Chinese Military Experience,* edited by Mike McDevitt and Mark Ryan (Armonk, New York: M. E. Sharpe Press, 2002).
8. Author's interview with Vietnamese foreign ministry officials, Hanoi, 1999.
9. "Hu Jintao Talks with Vietnamese Officials," Beijing Xinhua, Foreign Broadcast Information Service (hereafter FBIS) Daily Report, 17 December 1998.
10. "SRV Hails PRC Mine Clearing Operations along Border," Hanoi Voice of Vietnam, FBIS Daily Report, 14 August 1999.
11. Chinese foreign ministry spokeswoman Zhang Qiyue, on the announcement of the visit to Hanoi by Foreign Minister Tang Jiaxuan, 30 December 1999, *Beijing Review,* January 2000.
12. Dr. Tran Cong Truc, chairman of the Vietnamese Government Border Commission, "Official SRV-China Border Treaty," Hanoi *Tap Chi Quoc Phong Toan Dan,* 1 February 2000, 35–37.
13. Ibid. See also Carlyle Thayer, "China-ASEAN: Tensions Promote Discussions on a Code of Conduct," in *Comparative Connections* (First Quarter 2000): 54.
14. Vietnam and China held a seventh round of border talks in Beijing in February 2000 in which they "summed up the progress made in bilateral talks on border issues during the past year." Beijing Xinhua, FBIS Daily Report, 23 February 2000.
15. Thayer, "China-ASEAN"; Truc, "Official SRV-China Border Treaty." The then vice foreign minister Vu Khoan held discussions with Chinese foreign ministry officials in Beijing on 24 April 2000. Among the remaining irritants were a Chinese wall along the border in Quang Ninh Province, Chinese control of over 300 meters of railway north of Lang Son at the border, and resolution of the exact position of some border markers.
16. "Vietnam and China Sign Joint Statement in Beijing," Hanoi Vietnam News Agency (hereafter VNA), FBIS Daily Report, 25 December 2000.

17. "Jiang Zemin, Le Kha Phieu Confer," Beijing Xinhua, FBIS Daily Report, 25 February 1999.

18. "Vietnam, China Tonkin Gulf Working Group Meets," Hanoi VNA, FBIS Daily Report, 24 March 2000. See also "Vietnam, China Determine to Reach Tonkin Gulf Demarcation Agreement this Year," Hanoi VNA, FBIS Daily Report, 28 February 2000. Both sides reiterated their intention to conclude an agreement in 2000 after a meeting between Vietnamese foreign minister Nguyen Dy Nien and Chinese foreign minister Tang Jiaxuan.

19. Daniel J. Druzek, *Resource Disputes in the South China Sea*, Conference Paper for South China Sea Conference (Washington, D.C.: American Enterprise Institute, 7 September 1994).

20. Beijing *Muzi News*, FBIS Daily Report, 26 March 1999.

21. Beijing *Muzi News*, FBIS Daily Report, 21 January 2000; Department of Energy, Energy Information Administration, *Country Analysis: China* (Washington, D.C.), Internet version, accessed April 2001.

22. Beijing *People's Daily*, as referenced by Reuters, 16 August 1997. See also *Washington Times*, 21 March 1998, A6. Vietnam identified the rig as commencing drilling operations in its Block 113. The China National Offshore Oil Corporation reported that the rig, the Kantan III, was withdrawn "after completing its normal work." Agence France-Presse (hereafter AFP), as reported in the *South China Morning Post*, 8 April 1997.

23. Beijing *Muzi News*, FBIS Daily Report, 8 March 1999.

24. Vietnamese president Tran Duc Luong, in an interview with Moscow *Nezavisimaya Gazeta*, Interfax in English, FBIS Daily Report, 3 February 2000.

25. "Petro Vietnam Signs Oil Contract with American Company," Hanoi VNA, FBIS Daily Report, 28 January 2000; "Vietnam Oil Company Pumps 2.7 Million Tons of Crude Oil in Two Months," Hanoi VNA, FBIS Daily Report, 28 February 2000.

26. "Foreign Vessels Violate Fishing Grounds," Hanoi *Quan Doi Nhan Dan*, as reported by VNA, FBIS Daily Report, 8 May 1997.

27. Ibid.

28. Beijing *Muzi News*, FBIS Daily Report, 31 July 1998.

29. "Taking Advantage of China's Fishing Ban to Encroach upon its Fishing Areas," Guangzhou *Nanfang Ribao* (Internet version, accessed at <http://www.lateline.muzi .net, 16 January 2001) 21 July 1999.

30. Author discussions with maritime boundary experts at the University of Durham, the United Kingdom, February 2001.

31. Chinese foreign ministry spokesman Zhu Bangzao, as quoted by the Beijing *China Daily*, FBIS Daily Report, 14 February 2001.

32. Chien Chung, "Economic Development in the Islets of the South China Sea," AEI Conference Report, 9 September 1994, 6 and table 1.

33. Chang, *The Sino-Vietnamese Territorial Dispute*, 16; Philip Bowering, "The Balance of Power in the South China Sea," AEI Conference Report, 9 September 1994, 3–6.

34. Chang, *The Sino-Vietnamese Territorial Dispute*, 21–25.

35. Henry J. Kenny, "The South China Sea: A Dangerous Ground," *Naval War College Review* (Summer 1996).

36. Nguyen Hong Thao, "On China's Announcement of the Base Line for Use in Calculat-

ing the Width of Territorial Waters," Hanoi *Tap Chi Quoc Phong Toan Dan* 6 (June 1996).

37. "Declaration of the Government of the People's Republic of China on the Baseline of the Territorial Sea of the People's Republic of China," Beijing, 15 May 1996.

38. One of these is intended to measure earth crustal movement to help predict earthquakes. See "PRC Scientific Station in Paracels Becomes Operational," Beijing Xinhua, FBIS Daily Report, 27 December, 1999.

39. Nguyen Hong Thao, "China's New Advance into the Eastern Sea in 1998," Hanoi *Tap Chi Quoc Phong Toan Dan* (December 1998): 66–68.

40. Phan Thuy Thanh, Hanoi VNA, FBIS Daily Report, 2 June 1999. The spokeswoman affirmed Vietnam's sovereignty over the Hoang Sa and Truong Sa archipelagoes while answering correspondents' questions on Vietnam's stance on China's East Sea fishing ban from 1 June to 31 July 1999.

41. Beijing Xinhua, Guangzhou, 0246 GMT 12 April 2000.

42. Druzek, *Resource Disputes in the South China Sea*, table 1; CIA map, "The Spratly and Paracel Islands," 801947 (R001177), April 1992.

43. Thomas Johnson, "Opinion Reference Competing Claims of Vietnam and China in the Vanguard Bank and Blue Dragon Areas," (Covington and Burling, 27 January 1995), 11.

44. Marwyn Samuels, *Contest for the South China Sea* (New York: Methuen, 1982), 57. Because of this agreement, Chinese troops temporarily occupied the northern half of Vietnam.

45. Taiwan occupied Itu Aba in 1956 and maintained a small military garrison there until 1999, when it replaced it with Coast Guard personnel. Taiwan officials stated that the change resulted from fears that the increasing militarization of the Spratlys could lead to conflict with China. Author interview with Taiwan officials, 2000.

46. This was done by former premier Pham Van Dong.

47. "Saigon Says China Bombs Three Isles and Lands Troops," *New York Times,* 21 January 1974, A2; "Saigon Troops Reported on the Spratly Islands," *New York Times,* 1 February 1974, A8.

48. They were Southwest Cay, Gaven, Guarten Reefs, Fiery Cross, and Amboyan Cay. Samuels, *Contest for the South China Sea,* 20.

49. Michael Studeman, "Calculating China's Advances in the South China Sea," *Naval War College Review* (Spring 1988): 74–77.

50. Legislative Affairs Commission of the Standing Committee of the National People's Congress of the People's Republic of China, "Law of the People's Republic of China on the Territorial Sea and the Contiguous Zone" (Beijing: Science Press, 1992), 345–47.

51. "Declaration of the Government of the People's Republic of China on the Baseline of the Territorial Sea of the People's Republic of China," 16 May 1996, *Limits in the Seas, No. 117,* Office of Ocean Affairs, U.S. Department of State, 9 July 1996.

52. CIA map, "The Spratly and Paracel Islands," 801947 (R001177), April 1992; Pan Shiyang, Institute for International Technological Economic Studies, Beijing, in a paper prepared for AEI Conference on the South China Sea, 1994, 8. The number of Vietnamese-occupied islands has slowly risen in the past decade. See "Vietnam Holds Firm in Spratlys Dispute during Chi Haotian Visit," Hong Kong AFP, carried in the *South China Morning Post,* 10 February 2001.

53. *South China Morning Post,* "Vietnam Holds Firm in Spratlys Dispute during Chi Haotian Visit."

54. International Institute for Strategic Studies (IISS), *The Military Balance: 1999* (London, IISS: 2000), 201–202; Leonid Strezhevoy, "Overview of Vietnamese Armed Forces," Moscow *Nezavisimaya Gazeta,* 27 June 1996. See also "Naval Shipbuilding Programmes in Asia and the Middle East," *Naval Forces* (January 2000): 46.

55. "SRV Slams China's Move on Spratlys without SRV 'Consent,' " Hanoi Voice of Vietnam, FBIS Daily Report, 27 March 1999. Hanoi further declared: "Pending a long-term solution for the disputes, the parties concerned should try to maintain stability on the basis of the status quo, exercise self-restraint, and refrain from taking any action that will further complicate the situation while actively pushing negotiations to reach a fundamental and long-term solution to the disputes."

56. "Vietnam Affirms Claims over Spratlys, Paracels," Hanoi Voice of Vietnam, FBIS Daily Report, 7 January 1999.

57. Nguyen Hong Thao, "China's New Advance into the Eastern Sea in 1998."

58. Phan Thuy Thanh, 2 June 1999, as reported by Hanoi VNA, FBIS Daily Report, 2 June 1999.

59. "SRV Slams China's Move on Spratlys without SRV 'Consent,' " VNA.

60. Phan Thuy Thanh, "Hanoi Upholds Need to Agree on Sharing Mischief Reef," Hanoi VNA, FBIS Daily Report, 28 November 1998.

61. "Vietnam Refuses Direct Comment on Spratlys Shooting," Hong Kong AFP, FBIS Daily Report, 8 October 1999.

62. A Vietnamese government official involved in the negotiations, to the author, 1999.

63. In late 2000 the draft language was changed to the Spratlys and surrounding areas, leaving the question of whether the Paracels constituted surrounding areas as deliberately ambiguous. The Chinese, obviously, had taken a page from the Japanese Guidelines for Defense Cooperation with the United States, which used identical language with reference to Japanese support for U.S. forces in "areas surrounding Japan."

64. "Regional Code of Conduct in the South China Sea," and "Code of Conduct in the South China Sea," ASEAN and Chinese drafts respectively, provided to the author by an ASEAN member, March 2000.

65. Barry Wain, "A Code of Conduct in the South China Sea?" *Asian Wall Street Journal,* 10 March 2000.

66. Keun-Wook Paik and Duk-Ki Kim, "The Spratly Dispute and China's Naval Advance," *Geopolitics of Energy,* 1 October 1995; "Treacherous Shoals," *FEER,* 13 August 1992.

67. Henry J. Kenny, "The South China Sea: A Dangerous Ground," 97–99.

68. *Marine Petroleum,* as quoted by Nguyen Hong Thao, "China's New Advance into the Eastern Sea in 1998."

69. Hanoi VNA, FBIS Daily Report, 30 August 1999; "Oil, Gas, Mining," Special Report. Embassy of the Socialist Republic of Vietnam, Washington, D.C., 7 May 2000.

70. In April 2000 Hanoi approved a half billion dollar investment in a gas pipeline from the Con Son Basin to Vung Tau. Hanoi *Vietnam Economic Times,* May 2000. Gas production, meanwhile, has already begun. "The Bach Ho oil field supplies more than 4 million cubic meters of gas a day to the Ba Ria and Phu My electric power plants and the Dinh Co LPG"; Hanoi VNA, FBIS Daily Report, 30 August 1999.

71. Ibid., *Vietnam Economic Times.*

72. Phan Thuy Thanh, Vietnamese foreign ministry, as quoted in "China 'Slammed' for Pursuing Oil Deal in Spratly Islands." Hong Kong AFP, FBIS Daily Report, 5 September 1998; "SRV Reaffirms Sovereignty over Spratly, Paracel Islands," Hanoi, VNA, FBIS Daily Report, 4 September 1998.

73. Covington and Burling, "Opinion Reference Competing Claims of Vietnam and China in the Vanguard Bank and Blue Dragon Areas," 51–94. This opinion was prepared for the government of Vietnam.

74. Ibid.

75. "Overview of Vietnamese Armed Forces, Moscow *Nezavisimaya Gazeta,* June 1996; "Naval Shipbuilding Programs in Asia and the Far East," *Naval Forces 1/2000,* 48; the International Institute for Strategic Studies, *The Military Balance: 2000–2001* (London: Oxford University Press, 2001), 217–18.

76. For detail on Chinese and Vietnamese air capabilities, see *All the World's Aircraft, 1999–2000* (London: Janes Publishing Co., 2000).

77. Report by Vladimir Kucherenko, "Russia Seeks 'Energy Alliance' with PRC," Moscow *Rossiyskaya Gazeta,* 4 April 2000, 1, 7.

Chapter 5: Sino-Vietnamese Economic Relations

1. Tran Duc Luong, New Year Message, Hanoi *Nhan Dan,* 31 December 1999.

2. Poverty Working Group, The World Bank, Part 1: "Trends in Poverty," *Vietnam Attacking Poverty,* 1999. The slowdown in Vietnamese growth became apparent even before the Asian financial crisis.

3. Foreign direct investment commitments increased an average of $4.4 billion annually from 1991 to 1997. In 1998 that figure shrank to $1.7 billion. IMF Staff, *Country Report No. 99/55,* July 1999, table II-6.

4. From author's discussions with Vietnamese government officials, 1993–1996.

5. U.S. Arms Control and Disarmament Agency, *Worldwide Military Expenditures and Arms Transfers* (Washington, D.C.: U.S. Government Printing Office, 1996), table 1, p. 97. Gross national product per capita is in current dollars. The government of Vietnam claimed a per capita income of $220 in 1992. State Committee for Cooperation and Investment, *Investor's Guide* (New York: United Nations Industrial Development Organization, February 1994), 52.

6. The International Monetary Fund (IMF), *World Economic Outlook, Statistical Appendix* (Washington, D.C.: IMF, 1999), table 6: "Real GDP Growth: Developing Countries," for 1991 to 1998; Public Information Notice 99/46, "IMF Concludes Article IV Consultations with Vietnam," 8 June 1999; "Vietnam Statistical Appendix and Background Notes," IMF Staff Report 00/116, August 2000, 3. The IMF estimates Vietnamese GDP growth in 2000 at 5 percent. Higher oil production and prices, combined with increased government borrowing and expenditure, appeared to stimulate the slight rise in growth rate.

7. See, for example, the statement by Le Duc Thuy, governor of the IMF Fund for Vietnam, that "the financial crisis and economic recession and the complicated situation in the region and elsewhere are causing disadvantages on various sectors of our economy, especially export activity and foreign investment." Joint Annual Discussion of the Board of Governors of the International Monetary Fund, IMF Press Release No. 9, 29 September 1999.

8. These and other data on Chinese growth from 1978 to 1995 are analyzed in Vikram

Nehru, Aart Kraay, Xiaoqing Yu, et al., *China 2020: Development Challenges in the New Century* (Washington, D.C.: The World Bank, 1997).

9. Discussions by the author in Hanoi with officials of the Vietnamese foreign ministry, December 1994 and April 1977.

10. At the time Do Muoi, the general secretary of the Vietnamese Communist Party, launched a campaign to obliterate capitalism, stating, "Capitalists are like sewer rats; whenever one sees them popping up one must smash them to death." For this and further description of Vietnamese attitudes at the time, see Henry J. Kenny, "American Interests and Normalization with Vietnam, *The Aspen Quarterly* (Summer 1992).

11. Author's discussion with a Vietnamese government official, Hanoi, 1984.

12. *Vuon* refers to "garden," meaning that farmers could grow crops on private gardens around their houses; *ao* refers to "pond," the cultivation of fish in the numerous ponds throughout agricultural areas; and *truong* means "field," in which rice (at first only the yield above quota) could be sold at market prices. Author interviews with Vietnamese government officials, Hanoi, and visits to Vietnamese agricultural areas in the Red River Delta, October 1993.

13. Author's interviews with senior Vietnamese government officials in Hanoi, October 1993.

14. For example, the United Nations International Development Organization representative in Hanoi recently stated: "The Vietnamese are very keen to follow development in China." (Margot Cohen, *FEER*, 18 January 2001, 28–29.

15. Ho Chi Minh City *Saigon Times Daily*, FBIS Daily Report, 26 February 1999.

16. Hong Kong Zhongguo Tongxun She (China News Agency), 4 March 1999.

17. Beijing Xinhua, FBIS Daily Report, 2 March 1999. China actively encouraged Vietnamese delegations to emulate its socialist path. This was the meaning of Vice Premier and Foreign Minister Qian Qichen's quote of Mao that China should lean to one side (socialist side), Beijing *Renmin Ribao*, FBIS Daily Report, 25 September 1999.

18. "Li Kha Phieu Views Important Results of China Visit," Hanoi *Nhan Dan*, 4 March 1999.

19. Beijing Xinhua, FBIS Daily Report, 18 and 19 May 1999. Although reporting the visit, the Vietnamese media toned down the student-to-teacher nature of Dung's conversations with Chinese leaders. See, for example, "Nguyen Tan Dung Visits China 18 May to Study PRC Reform," Hanoi VNA, FBIS Daily Report, 20 May 1999.

20. Deputy Minister of the State Planning Commission Liu Jiang repaid Vietnam the compliment. Beijing Xinhua, FBIS Daily Report, 7 July 1999.

21. Hanoi Voice of Vietnam Network, FBIS Daily Report, 27 September 1999.

22. Beijing Xinhua, FBIS Daily Report, 27 September 1999.

23. Hanoi VNA, FBIS Daily Report, 1 October 1999. See also Beijing Xinhua, FBIS Daily Report, 10 October 1999. These comments were typical of Xinhua representation of official Vietnamese groups visiting Beijing. For example, in April 1999 Politburo member Jia Qinglin met with the Vietnamese Fatherland Front secretary-general Tran Van Dang (transcribed by Xinhua as Chen Wen Deng), who was quoted as seeing "China's tremendous and profound changes and learned about the successful experiences of party and government of China in economic development." Beijing Xinhua, 21 April 1999.

24. Senior Lieutenant General Pham Van Tra, "Chi Haotian Holds Talks with Vietnamese Counterpart," Beijing Xinhua, FBIS Daily Report, 8 February 2001.

25. Ibid.; "Vietnam Pays Great Attention to China's Experience: Party Leader," Beijing Xinhua, FBIS Daily Report, 9 February 2001.

26. The reference here is to the revolutionary appeal of Phan Boi Chau that Vietnam must learn from Japan, which had defeated the Russian fleet off Tshushima Strait in 1905. When Ho asked how Japan had realized its technological achievements, Chau replied that the Japanese had learned from the West. Ho thereupon rejected Chau's strategy, stating he preferred to go to the source to see the secret of Western success. Duiker, Ho Chi Minh, 26–27.

27. Hanoi VNA, FBIS Daily Report, 18 December 1998, and Beijing Xinhua, FBIS Daily Report, 18 December 1998.

28. Because Zhu Rongji was on a foreign visit, Phieu met with Li. Beijing Xinhua, FBIS Daily Report, 26 February 1999.

29. Hanoi Voice of Vietnam, FBIS Daily Report, 17 December 1998.

30. Hanoi VNA, FBIS Daily Report, 1 June 1999; BBC, 17 September 1999. Another example is Chinese assistance for Vietnamese forestry, valued at $4.6 million in 1999. Ho Chi Minh City The Saigon Times, FBIS Daily Report, 17 December 1999; Lang Son–Guangxi postal service was also restored. Hanoi VNA, FBIS Daily Report, 5 August 1999.

31. Chinese assistant foreign minister Wang Yi, Beijing Xinhua, FBIS Daily Report, 17 March 1999.

32. Hanoi Voice of Vietnam, FBIS Daily Report, 17 December 1998.

33. Beijing Xinhua, FBIS Daily Report, 26 February 1999.

34. Beijing Xinhua, FBIS Daily Report, 15 May 1999.

35. Hong Kong China News Agency, 24 October 1998. The news agency incorrectly referred to Luong as CPV chairman.

36. Hong Kong China News Agency, 4 March 1999.

37. Beijing Xinhua, FBIS Daily Report, 26 February 1999.

38. IMF Staff Report 99/55, 10.

39. Ibid., "Vietnam: Selected Issues," table II-4, July 1999. Based on author's discussions with the staff of the planning and investment ministry, the State Bank of Vietnam, and the finance ministry, the IMF has discounted official Vietnamese figures for total reported loans by one-third. Data is from the beginning of significant FDI in 1988 through 1998. Data for China is from London BBC, FBIS Daily Report, 19 October 1998.

40. Hong Kong China News Agency, 24 October 1998.

41. Hanoi Voice of Vietnam, FBIS Daily Report, 19 July 1999.

42. IMF Staff Report 99/55, 10.

43. Hanoi VNA, as monitored by the BBC, News Agency Highlights, "Sino-Vietnamese Economic Ties," 25 November 1999.

44. United Nations Development Program (UNDP) and Vietnamese Ministry of Planning and Investment, "Bilateral Donors," December 1999; and UNDP, "Overview of Official Development Assistance in Vietnam," Hanoi, December 1999, 10.

45. Named after former prime minister and then finance minister Kiichi Miyazawa, the plan pledged $30 billion for the recovery of the economies of Asia, originally limited to Indonesia, Thailand, the Philippines, Malaysia, and South Korea.

46. Vietnamese deputy trade minister Nguyen Xuan Quang, in an address to the Enterprises Forum, as reported by Hanoi VNA, FBIS Daily Report, 29 September 1999.

47. The figures from which these points were derived are from the Economic Intelligence Unit (EIU), *Vietnam Country Report* (London: EIU, 2000), fourth quarter, 1999, 4–6 and 35; UNDP, *Vietnam Socio-Economic Statistical Bulletin,* February 2000, part 1.

48. Hanoi VNA, FBIS Daily Report, 1 December 1999. Khai said that both countries seek to attain a goal of $2 billion in two-way trade in 2000.

49. Ho Chi Minh City *Saigon Times* reported the Chinese foreign exchange reserves at $150 billion, 1 October 1999.

50. Hanoi VNA, FBIS Daily Report, 29 August 1999.

51. Pham Van Khai, to ASEAN Summit Conference, Hanoi Vietnam Television Network, FBIS Daily Report, 17 December 1998.

52. Hong Kong AFP, FBIS Daily Report, 20 October 1999; "Composition of China's Imports from Vietnam," *China Economic Information,* Beijing, 29 June 1999; observations from author's visit to Bat Trang, October 1993.

53. Hong Kong *South China Morning Post,* 24 October 1999; Ho Chi Minh City *Saigon Times,* 28 October 1999; Hanoi VNA, FBIS Daily Report, 15 July 1999.

54. Hong Kong China News Agency, 4 March 1999. There are 12 points of entry and 25 mutual markets along the border; Beijing Xinhua, Hong Kong Service, FBIS Daily Report, 6 December 1998.

55. Hanoi VNA, FBIS Daily Report, 23 July 1999.

56. Hanoi VNA, FBIS Daily Report, 12 September 1999.

57. "Customs Nabs Three Smuggling Vessels, Sinks One," Beijing Zhongguo Xinwen She, FBIS Daily Report, 7 January 1999.

58. Wu Yi, as quoted by Hong Kong *Ming Pao,* "Nationwide Antismuggling Campaign," 28 September 1998. China appears to have adopted a policy of reducing tariffs as another way to combat smuggling. In 1999 Hainan reduced tariffs on Vietnamese imports to only half of that imposed on other countries. As a result, Vietnamese trade with Hainan has tripled from its very low base in 1998. Beijing Xinhua, FBIS Daily Report, 24 May 1999.

59. Hong Kong *Hsin Pao,* FBIS Daily Report, 23 October 1998.

60. "Nationwide Major Antismuggling Campaign," Hong Kong *Ming Pao,* FBIS Daily Report, 28 September 1998.

61. Hong Kong *South China Morning Post,* FBIS Daily Report, 29 December 1999.

62. "Interviews Phan Van Khai on PRC Anniversary," Beijing Xinhua, FBIS Daily Report, 27 September 1999.

63. Ibid. Although Vietnam never created segregated communes like China, it did collectivize agriculture, establish quotas, and disallow the sale of agricultural products at market prices. It established over 10,000 collectives *(xa)* in Vietnam's 61 provinces. *Danh Muc Cac Don Vi Hanh Chinh Vietnam* (Vietnam's List of Administrative Divisions) (Hanoi: Nha Xuat Ban Thong Ke, 2000).

64. *China 2020: Development Challenges in the New Century* (Washington, D.C.: The World Bank, 1997), 3.

65. From author's meetings with Vietnamese officials in Hanoi, January 1999.

66. Pham Van Khai, to ASEAN Summit Conference, Hanoi Vietnam Television Network, 17 December 1998.

67. "Address to the 10th National Assembly, fourth session, October 1998," Hanoi Vietnam Television Network, 28 October 1998.

68. Moscow Interfax, *Daily Financial Report*, FBIS Daily Report, 27 August 1999.

69. Thirty companies are operating off Vietnam's continental shelf. Moscow *Nezavisimaya Gazeta*, 3 December 1999, as reported by BBC, 12 December 1999.

70. Japan's trade with Vietnam in 1998 totaled over $3 billion, compared to Chinese trade of just over a $1.2 billion. EIU, *Country Report: China*, 33.

71. See, for example, the remarks of National Assembly chairman Nong Duc Manh, thanking Japan for its assistance. Hanoi VNA, FBIS Daily Report, 20 September 1999.

72. Hanoi Vietnam Television Network, 28 October 1998.

73. IMF Report 99/55, table II.4; EIU, *Country Report: China*, 33.

74. David Hsu, Taipei Taiwan Central News Agency, 4 April 1999; Ho Chi Minh City *Saigon Times*, 10 September 1999.

75. Hung Tun-jen, Director of Taiwan External Trade Development Council, 18 April 1999. Taipei Taiwan Central News Agency, 4 and 29 October 1999.

76. Beijing Xinhua, FBIS Daily Report, 26 July 1999.

77. Carlyle A. Thayer, comments at the Pacific Forum, Hawaii, August 1999.

78. During the early 1990s, PAVN had turned to the PLA practice of commerce to finance its modernization. Anthony Salzman, of the U.S. Chamber of Commerce in Vietnam, said Vietnam's reluctance to implement the trade agreement was "very disappointing." Hong Kong *South China Morning Post*, 14 September 1999.

79. Hong Kong *South China Morning Post*, 14 December 1999.

Chapter 6: The Politics of Sino-Vietnamese Relations

1. The Vietnamese position on the South China Sea is the major exception to this posture.

2. According to former South Vietnamese premier Nguyen Cao Ky, this sealed the fate of South Vietnam. He compared the war to a football game in which the Washington-Saigon side was not allowed to cross the 50-yard line. Discussions at West Point, New York, 1972. It is also worth noting that U.S. policy prohibited air attacks on North Vietnam within 25 miles of the China border.

3. Henry J. Kenny, "Vietnamese Perceptions of the 1979 War with China." Vietnam lost a similar number.

4. According to the author Qiang Zhai, there were 130,000 Chinese soldiers in North Vietnam in 1966, a figure that later rose to nearly 200,000. Qiang Zhai, *China and the Vietnam Wars, 1950–1975* (Chapel Hill, N.C.: University of North Carolina Press, 2000).

5. Vietnam reformers refrained from invoking China as a model, even though they knew of its success, because of the 1979 war and its aftermath. At the time, Vietnam vowed to hold tight to strict socialist doctrine and not follow the Chinese model.

6. These changes were codified in Politburo Resolution nos. 2 and 13 of 1987 and 1988 respectively. Carlyle A. Thayer and Ramses Amer, eds., *Vietnamese Foreign Policy in Transition* (New York: St. Martin's Press, 1999), 2.

7. Normalization was explored at lower levels in 1988 and 1989, but the first top-level dialogue occurred in 1990, when Vietnamese general secretary Nguyen Van Linh met with his counterpart, Jiang Zemin, at Chengdu, the provincial capital of Sichuan. The two leaders reached a preliminary agreement on normalization at that time.

Author discussions with senior Vietnamese officials in Hanoi, 1999; and "Viewing Sino-Vietnamese Relations from Vietnamese Prime Minister's Recent Visit," Hong Kong Zhongguo Tongxun She (China News Agency), 24 October 1998.

8. Nayan Chanda, "Friend or Foe?" *FEER*, 22 June 2000, 32.

9. See chapters 4 and 5. Vietnamese officials expressed concern to the author regarding the overall Chinese military buildup.

10. Interviews with Vietnamese government officials, 1999.

11. Hans Morgenthau, *Politics among Nations,* 4th edition (New York: Alfred A. Knopf, 1967), 161–215.

12. See chapter 4. The land border agreement appeared to have some difficulties in implementation as the Vietnam-China Border Demarcation Joint Committee met for the second time in Hanoi during the second half of February 2001. During a February 2001 visit to Hanoi, Chinese defense minister Chi Haotian and his Vietnamese counterpart, Pham Van Tra, agreed "to strive to turn the common border into a peaceful, stable, friendly border," implying that it was not such a border at the time. See Carlyle Thayer, "Regional Rivalries and Bilateral Irritants," *Comparative Connections* (1st Quarter, 2001).

13. Interview with Vietnamese government official, 1999.

14. Nguyen Manh Hung, "Vietnam in 1999," *Asian Survey* (January 2000): 106.

15. *China Economic Daily, Jingi Ribao,* as quoted in Asia Intelligence Wire, 26 February 1999.

16. Vietnamese officials indicated to the author that the Chinese were not yielding on any points in difficult discussions on the Tonkin Gulf and the South China Sea. A senior official stated that, with China pushing its claims in the South China Sea, Vietnam is not in a strategic position to deal with the situation, and that China has seized upon the shift in balance of power in the region. Author's discussions with Vietnamese officials in Hanoi and Washington, D.C., 1999.

17. "The Positive Results of Le Kha Phieu Highly Appraised," Hong Kong China News Agency, 4 March 1999; "Sino-Vietnamese Relations Facing the 21st Century," *Beijing Review,* 15–21 March 1999, 7–8. There is some indication both leaders discussed ways to maintain party control. Beijing Xinhua, FBIS Daily Report, 25 February 1999. Phieu also went to Beijing to reassure China about the March 2000 visit by U.S. defense secretary William Cohen. Chanda, "Friend or Foe?" 32.

18. Li Lanqing Meets Le Kha Phieu," Beijing Xinhua, FBIS Daily Report, 26 February 1999.

19. Chanda, "Friend or Foe?" 32.

20. Liu Yunfei, Beijing Xinhua, FBIS Daily Report, 21 April 1999.

21. "SRV Fatherland Front Receives Chinese Guest," Hanoi Voice of Vietnam, FBIS Daily Report, 30 August 1999; "Foreign Delegates Hail SRV Front Congress," Hanoi VNA, FBIS Daily Report, 28 August 1999; "Chinese People's Consultative Official on Ties with the SRV," FBIS Daily Report, 25 September 1999.

22. "Li Ruihuan Meets Vietnamese Communist Party Official," Beijing Xinhua, FBIS Daily Report, 9 October 1999.

23. See, for example, comments by Chinese premier Zhu Rongji to Vietnamese prime minister Phan Van Khai in Beijing, Beijing Xinhua, FBIS Daily Report, 25 September 2000.

24. The visit was made from 24 to 27 February 2000. Thayer, "China-ASEAN," 54.

25. Carlyle A. Thayer, "China Consolidates Its Long-term Bilateral Relations with South-east Asia," *Comparative Connections* (2d Quarter 2000): 8; Chanda, "Friend or Foe?" 32. The Vietnamese delegation then traveled to southwest China and was promised $55 million for economic reconstruction in border regions.

26. "Chinese President Jiang Zemin Meets Vietnamese Prime Minister on Border Issues," Beijing Xinhua, FBIS Daily Report, 26 September 2000; "PRC's Li Peng Meets Vietnamese Prime Minister on Economic, Social Cooperation," Beijing Xinhua, FBIS Daily Report, 26 September 2000.

27. This and the preceding point are cited in Thayer, "China's New Security Concept and ASEAN."

28. "Hu Jintao, Vietnamese President Discuss Friendly Relationship," Beijing Xinhua, FBIS Daily Report, 19 April 2001; "Chinese Vice President Hu Jintao Interviewed on Ties with Vietnam," Hanoi VNA, FBIS Daily Report, 22 April 2001.

29. "Viewing Sino-Vietnamese Relations from Vietnamese Prime Minister's Recent Visit," Hong Kong China News Agency, 24 October 1998.

30. Nayan Chanda, "Pulled Two Ways," *FEER,* 26 August 1999, 25. I found similar attitudes in meetings with some Vietnamese officials, but as stated below, these views were by no means unanimous.

31. For example, in their October 1999 meeting in Beijing, Chinese defense minister Chi Haotian and Lieutenant General Doan Chuong, president of Vietnam's Institute of Military Strategy, stressed the importance of army building to enhance their national defense against "hostile forces." The February 2001 meetings between defense ministers stressed military cooperation and Vietnamese admiration for China's opening up.

32. "Vietnamese Minister Attends Chinese Army Day Reception," Hanoi VNA, FBIS Daily Report, 30 July 1999.

33. "Landmines Cleared from Yunnan in Model Operation," Hong Kong *South China Morning Post,* 27 March 1999.

34. EIU, *Country Report: Vietnam* (4th Quarter 1998): 14.

35. The People's Army of Vietnam has a reported strength of 492,000, down from 1.3 million in 1987, while the PLA recently reduced its force by 500,000. Vietnamese and Chinese White Papers on Defense, 1998 and 2000 respectively.

36. Author interviews with senior PAVN officers, Hanoi, 1999.

37. "Vietnam: New Party Leader Nong Duc Manh Meets Pressmen," Hanoi VNA, FBIS Daily Report, 22 April 2001.

38. For an excellent description of Vietnamese motivation in joining ASEAN, see Carlyle A. Thayer, "Vietnamese Foreign Policy: Multilateralism and the Threat of Peaceful Evolution," in Thayer and Amer, *Vietnamese Foreign Policy in Transition,* 1–20.

39. Although favoring the opening to ASEAN, Do Muoi wanted to restrict ASEAN influence in Vietnam. He once made the statement that "capitalists are like sewer rats; whenever one sees them popping up one must smash them to death." Kenny, "American Interests and Normalization with Vietnam," 51. Interestingly, Dao Duy Tung's brother, Dao Duy Chu, is an entrepreneur with considerable business acumen. Author's meetings with Chu on potential business deals for a U.S. company, Hanoi and Saigon, 1994.

40. "Strengthening Sino-Vietnamese Relations to Move Toward the 21st Century," Hanoi *Nhan Dan,* FBIS Daily Report, 18 October 1998.

41. An example of the ASEAN reaction was the statement by Abu Bakr Daud of Malaysia, then chairman of the committee, that the ASEAN nations appreciated China's efforts to assist in their recovery. "ASEAN-PRC Joint Committee Meeting Opens," Beijing Xinhua, FBIS Daily Report, 17 March 1999.

42. "Vietnam Official Hails ASEAN Ministerial Success," Hanoi VNA, FBIS Daily Report, 29 July 1999.

43. "China to Sign Southeast Asia's Anti-Nuclear Treaty," Kuala Lumpur *Star,* 28 July 1999.

44. Carlyle A. Thayer, "China Consolidates Its Long-term Bilateral Relations with Southeast Asia, 2–3 and 7–8.

45. "Security Cooperation Among ASEAN Countries," Hong Kong *Ta Kung Pao,* quoting Lu Jianren of the Chinese Academy of Social Sciences, FBIS Daily Report, 7 July 1999.

46. "Economic Council Head Leaves for Vietnam," Taipei Taiwan Central News Agency, FBIS Daily Report, 22 April 1999.

47. EIU, *Country Report: Vietnam* (April 2000): 5 and 36.

48. EIU, *Country Report: Vietnam* (2d Quarter 1999): 31.

49. "Russia and Vietnam Sign Cooperation Accord," Beijing Xinhua, FBIS Daily Report, 2 July 1999.

50. "Russian Journalist Says Putin's Foreign Policy Success Nothing but PR Stunt," Moscow Ekho Moskvy Radio, FBIS Daily Report, 4 March 2001.

51. Author conversations with Vietnamese officials in Hanoi, 1993, 1994, and 1999.

52. David Halberstam, *Ho* (New York: Vintage Books, 1971), 74.

53. Chanda, "Friend or Foe," 32. The agreement, reached on 25 July 1999, was expected to be formally signed at the Asia Pacific Economic Cooperation summit in New Zealand in September, but was not signed until seven months later.

54. Ibid. for the secret Phieu visit. After the bombing, Vietnam immediately sent a message to China condemning the incident as a "violation of international law," a "barbarian action." It expressed condolences to the victims and demanded an immediate end to NATO bombing in Yugoslavia. See, for example, "Vietnam Foreign Minister Condemns NATO Attack on Chinese Embassy," 10 May 1999, and "Vietnam Organizations Condemn Attack on Embassy," Beijing Xinhua, FBIS Daily Report, 13 May 1999. Vietnam continued to support China fully on this incident. In the same month of the second scheduled Cohen visit, Vietnamese foreign minister Nguyen Manh Cam, who was considered friendly toward the United States, stated before the United Nations General Assembly that "the unilateral military attacks (of the United States) against sovereign states and their territorial integrity in the Balkans and the Persian Gulf have set a dangerous precedent in international relations, running counter to the UN principles and objectives, violating fundamental principles of international law, and seriously challenging the role and mandate of this organization and its legal foundations." Nguyen Manh Cam Address at the 54th UN General Assembly, September 26, 1999.

55. Author interview with Vietnamese official, 1999.

56. Duong Thu Huong, *Paradise of the Blind* (Penguin, 1994); *A Novel without a Name* (Hyperion, 1994); *Memories of a Pure Spring* (Hyperion, 2000); *Beyond Illusions* (William Murrow, forthcoming 2002).

57. EIU, *Country Report: Vietnam* (2d Quarter 1999): 12.

58. EIU, *Country Report: Vietnam* (3d Quarter 1998): 12.

59. EIU, *Country Report: Vietnam* (1st Quarter 1999): 11–12; EIU, *Country Report: Vietnam,* April 2000, 14.

60. Ibid., April 2000, 13.

61. Reporting from Hanoi, Huw Watkin presents a graphic illustration of this phenomenon in "Vietnam's Misspent Youth," Hong Kong *South China Morning Post,* 19 September 1999. The Vietnamese campaign was approved at the second session of the party Central Committee's sixth plenum, 25 January through 2 February 1999; it was launched in May 1999 with a two-year target date for completion. Its stated purpose is to attack the "four dangers" of (1) corruption, (2) economic backwardness, (3) deviation from socialist path, and (4) threat of peaceful evolution. One of the first targets of the reform was Deputy Prime Minister Nguyen Xuan Loc, a reformer, who was removed from office and the party for alleged corruption. *FEER,* 9 December 1999, 26; EIU, *Country Report: Vietnam* (1st Quarter 2000): 12.

62. Margot Cohen, "Passing the Buck," *FEER,* 7 December 2000.

63. For example, Nguyen Hoang Linh, former editor of *Doanh Nghiep* (Enterprise), was arrested in 1998 for articles alleging corruption. EIU, *Country Report: Vietnam* (4th Quarter 1998): 13. In an October 1999 article in *Saigon Giai Phong,* Tran Trong Tan, a former senior party member, accused the party leadership of "looking down on the people." EIU, *Country Report: Vietnam* (1st Quarter 2000): 8.

64. Nayan Chanda, *FEER,* 4 May 2000, 20.

65. Susan V. Lawrence, reporting from Beijing, "China: A City Ruled by Crime," *New York Times,* 30 November 2000. See also Bruce Gilley, "Fallen Idol," *FEER,* 18 November 1999, 22; "Corruption Hurts Credibility of Chinese Communist Party," EIU, *Country Report: China* (2d Quarter 1999): 13.

66. Ibid., p. 11; EIU, *Country Report: Vietnam* (1st Quarter 2000).

67. Huw Watkin, "Vietnam's Misspent Youth," 14.

68. Elected People's Councils in Vietnam typically find themselves subservient to People's Committees appointed by the party. The same applies to China. *Washington Post,* 26 August 2000, 1; EIU, *Country Report: Vietnam* (4th Quarter 1998): 7.

69. Party members clearly benefit from the reforms. Many have become rich because they control the means of production. Their incentive is to maintain their political and economic power base, while extending the reforms countrywide only insofar as they can maintain at least some control of them.

70. Huw Watkin, "Vietnam's Misspent Youth."

71. EIU, *Country Report: Vietnam* (April 2000): 18.

72. The World Bank reported in 1999 that it took $18,000 in investment to create a new job in an SOE, compared to $800 for a private company. EIU, *Country Report: Vietnam* (2d Quarter 1999): p. 20. The bank stated "the SOEs will make more losses pile up and more non-repayable bank debt, thereby worsening the quality of bank assets further." Hong Kong *South China Morning Post,* 14 December 1999. See also Bruce Gilley, "China's Bankers: Rotten to the Top," *FEER* 31 January 2002.

73. Mark Landler, "China Web Rules Limits Foreigners," *New York Times,* 21 November 2000; Mark Landler, "Rolling with China's Web Punches," *New York Times,* 31 January 2001.

74. Lorien Holland, *FEER,* 2 December 1999, 44.

75. For a detailed explanation of Chinese commitments under the WTO, see Legal Support Services, Ltd., "WTO Accession," Internet version available as of December 2001 at http://www.chinalegalchange.com, which provides details of every aspect of Chinese commitments from May 2000 to October 2001.

76. Web access costs $1.20 an hour plus steep phone charges. Universities are attempting to make it free to students, but the process is likely to be slow. "Like China Vietnam's communist regime fears the political implications of information technology." Margot Cohen, "Free to Surf," *FEER*, 13 April 2000.

77. "China and Vietnam Sign Tourism Agreement," Beijing Xinhua, FBIS Daily Report, 7 April 1999. See also *FEER* 17 January 2002.

78. At times, Vietnam sought alternatives, principally in its march south into Champa and the Mekong Delta, but was extremely suspicious of modernization along Western lines, as it is today.

79. See chapter 2 for details. A former government official told the author: "We had to fight 13 wars with China in our history. Our ancestors knew how to fight back against China. We must likewise be prepared. Our ancestors also knew how to preclude war. We must take similar steps in the future."

Chapter 7: American Interests and the Future of Sino-Vietnamese Relations

1. See NSC 48/5, approved by the president on 17 May 1951; *Pentagon Papers, Volume 8*, (Washington, D.C.: U.S. Government Printing Office, 1973), 423–26.

2. Lyndon B. Johnson, *The Vantage Point: Perspectives of the Presidency, 1963–1969* (New York: Holt, Rinehart, and Winston, 1971), 136.

3. The Vietnam-United States Trade Agreement, signed by U.S. and Vietnamese negotiators on 13 July 2000, required approval by both the U.S. Congress and the Vietnamese National Assembly. Because of the November 2000 general election and a tight congressional schedule that included extensive debate over permanent normal trade relations with China, the Clinton administration decided not to submit the agreement to the 106th Congress.

4. As part of the agreement, Vietnam consented to a wide range of measures to improve market access for U.S. exports and investments. It committed Vietnam to 200 specific pledges over its first five years, including reducing its tariffs on U.S. exports; opening its service sector, especially insurance and banking; and protecting intellectual property rights. For further details, see Mark E. Manyin, "The Vietnam-U.S. Bilateral Trade Agreement," Congressional Research Service, 21 July 2000. See also EIU, *Country Report: Vietnam* (1st Quarter 2000): 14.

5. Manyin, "The Vietnam-U.S. Bilateral Trade Agreement"; EIU, *Country Report: Vietnam* (4th Quarter 1999) and (April 2000): 16 and 15 respectively. There was a report that the Vietnamese negotiators were not speaking with one voice.

6. EIU, *Country Report: Vietnam* (4th Quarter 1999); Adrian Edwards, "Closed Minds," *FEER*, 9 December 1999. The World Bank estimate was $800 million. Average U.S. tariffs would fall from 40 percent to less than 3 percent.

7. Nayan Chanda, "Hanoi Deal on Ice," Intelligence Section, *FEER*, 6 April 2000, p. 9; Chanda, "Friend or Foe?" 32.

8. Hung, "Vietnam in 1999," 107–108. The U.S. consulate opened on 16 August 1999.

9. Susan Lawrence, "Yearning to Lead," *FEER*, 3 and 16 September 1999. Vietnam and China also joined in condemning Senate action in rejecting the Comprehensive Test Ban Treaty, Hanoi *Nhan Dan*, 13 October 1999.

10. The White Paper strongly criticized the U.S. military presence and referred to the United States as a "hegemon" over a dozen times. In March 2000 the Chinese Institute of Contemporary International Relations called for regional alliances between China and several Asian countries to oppose the U.S. military presence in Asia. Chronology of China-ASEAN Relations, Contemporary International Relations, the Asia-Pacific Center for Security Studies.

11. Hung, "Vietnam in 1999," 107; Thayer, "Regional Rivalries and Bilateral Irritants," 14.

12. See chapters 5 and 6 for analysis of the summit.

13. Thayer, "Regional Rivalries and Bilateral Irritants," 13; Nayan Chanda, "Pulled Two Ways," *FEER*, 26 August 1999, 24.

14. Jiang condemned "the new gunboat diplomacy" and neocolonialism pursued by some big powers. Claiming the moral high ground, Chinese spokesmen, followed by Vietnamese spokesmen, denounced the U.S. attack on the PRC embassy. The Vietnamese used much the same language as the Chinese, referring to the bombing as a deliberate act and interference in the internal affairs of other nations. See, for example, "Hanoi Radio Denounces NATO Attack on PRC Embassy in Belgrade," Hanoi Voice of Vietnam, FBIS Daily Report, 20 October 1999; and Nguyen Manh Cam, in an address to the United Nations General Assembly, 25 September 1999, as reported by Hanoi VNA, FBIS Daily Report, 26 September 1999.

15. EIU, *Country Report: Vietnam* (April 2000): 16; Hung, "Vietnam in 1999," 108. Vietnam did, however, agree to conduct military cooperation with Russia and South Korea—both South Korean and Japanese naval vessels visited Vietnam in 1999.

16. *Washington Post*, 16 January 2001; Chanda, "Cam Ranh Bay Manoeuvers," *FEER*, 4 January 2001, 21–23. A spokesperson for the foreign ministry was quoted as saying: "At this point in time we are tied up with other work which could not be delayed, so we propose postponing the visit." Reuters, Hanoi, 16 January 2001. No date has been set for a rescheduled Blair visit.

17. Hanoi canceled Admiral Blair's visit while he was in Kuala Lumpur, his last scheduled stop before leaving for Vietnam. The foreign ministry stated that "Vietnam welcomes the visit but at the moment Vietnam is so engaged and proposes delaying the visit to a more relevant time." Hanoi Voice of Vietnam News, FBIS Daily Report, 16 January 2001. Vietnam had no trouble accommodating two Russian ships on a visit to Cam Ranh Bay in March.

18. For example, former president Bill Clinton upon signing the bilateral trade agreement with Vietnam, stated: "We hope trade will go hand in hand with strength and respect for human rights and labor standards. For we live in an age where wealth is generated by the free exchange of ideas and stability depends on democratic choices." "Remarks by the President," Office of the Press Secretary, The White House, 11 July 1995, on normalization and 13 July 2000.

19. Ibid.

20. Nayan Chanda, "Blowing Hot and Cold," *FEER*, 30 November 2000, 24–25.

21. These are the Gulf of Tonkin, the Paracel Islands, the Spratly Islands, and the Con Son Basin. After Indonesia rejected Chinese claims to the fifth area, the Natuna field, Exxon and Pertamina initiated a $40 billion investment in its development.

22. Gene Sperling, director of the National Economic Council, 18 May 2000.

23. According to senior Vietnamese officials, Washington gave the green light to Beijing when Deng Xiaoping told President Jimmy Carter that China would have "to teach Vietnam a lesson" by attacking Vietnam. Meeting with Vietnamese officials, 1999.

24. United States Energy Information Administration, "South China Sea Region," January 2000.

25. This is especially the case if other Asian nations were to join with China in a quasi-alliance, such as the former Beijing-Hanoi-Jakarta-Pyongyang axis cited earlier.

26. The time differential, however, need not be nearly as long. China enjoyed normal trade relations with the United States for over a decade before Vietnam did.

27. U.S. Department of State, "Vietnam: Human Rights Reports for 1999" (Washington, D.C.: Department of State, 2000). Vietnam bridled at the report.

28. Ho Chi Minh proclaimed the Democratic Republic of Vietnam in 1946. After its victory over the Republic of Vietnam in 1975, Hanoi changed the word "Democratic" to "Socialist." Ho at least recognized the Vietnamese love for democracy in the original title, and in his famous quote: *"Khong co gi quy hon doc lap, tu do"* (there is nothing more precious than independence and freedom). Unfortunately, he and his successors seem to have forgotten the latter part of that phrase.

29. See Margot Cohen, "Free to Surf," *FEER,* 13 April 2000. Web costs are $1.20 per hour. The Vietnamese Ministry of Post and Telecommunications maintains control of the international gateway.

30. The one-year lag in executing the agreement on normal trade relations was, as indicated earlier, partly the result of Vietnam's acting in deference to China. Vietnamese officials expressed fears that U.S. policy is driving China and Russia together, thereby strengthening Chinese military power. They also indicated that they do not want the United States to use Vietnam as a "card" against China. Author's interviews with Vietnamese officials.

31. For more detailed analysis of potential disruption of these sea-lanes, see Henry J. Kenny, *Possible Threats to Shipping in Key Southeast Asian Sea Lanes* (Alexandria, Va.: Center for Naval Analyses, 1996). See also John H. Noer, *Maritime Interests in the Sea Lines of Communication through the South China Sea* (Washington, D.C.: National Defense University Press, 1997).

32. Deliberations under the ASEAN Regional Forum generally exclude the United States. U.S. representatives regularly meet with the concerned foreign ministry officials of the ASEAN states and express support for their consensus-building measures initiatives, but the official U.S. role is limited. U.S. experts, however, are involved in Track II efforts to maintain peace in disputed areas.

33. The Space Research Institute at the George Washington University completed a test program in 2000 that shows that commercial satellites can monitor ship movements and military construction in the Spratlys. Commercial satellites can now produce imagery down to one-meter resolution.

SELECT BIBLIOGRAPHY

Books

Abuza, Zachary M. "Coping with China: Vietnam Elite Responses to an Emerging Super-power." Ph.D. Dissertation, Fletcher School of Law and Diplomacy, 1998.

Bui Tin. *Following Ho Chi Minh, Memoirs of A North Vietnamese Colonel.* New South Wales, Australia: Crawford House, 1992.

Buttinger, Joseph. *A Dragon Defiant: A Short History of Vietnam.* New York: Praeger, 1972.

———. *Vietnam: A Political History.* New York: Praeger, 1968.

Cady, John F. *Southeast Asia: Its Historical Development.* New York: McGraw-Hill, 1964.

Cameron Allan W., ed. *Vietnam Crisis—A Documentary History, Volume 1: 1940–1956.* Ithaca, N.Y.: Cornell University Press, 1971.

Chanda, Nayan. *Brother Enemy: The War after the War—A History of Indochina since the Fall of Saigon.* Orlando, Fla.: Harcourt Brace Jovanovich, 1986.

Chang, Pao-min. *The Sino-Vietnamese Territorial Dispute.* Washington, D.C.: Center for Strategic and International Studies, 1986.

Chapuis, H. Oscar. *A History of Vietnam from Hong Bang to Tu Duc.* London: Greenwood Press, 1995.

———. *The Last Emperors of Vietnam: From Tu Duc to Bao Dai.* Westwood, Conn.: Greenwood Press, 2000.

Chen, King C. *China's War with Vietnam, 1979: Issues, Decisions, and Implications.* Stanford, Calif.: Hoover Institution Press, 1987.

———. *Vietnam and China, 1938–1954.* Princeton, N.J.: Princeton University Press, 1969.

Department of Defense. *The Pentagon Papers, U.S.-Vietnam Relations, 1945–1967.* Washington, D.C.: U.S. Government Printing Office, 1971.

Duiker, William J. *China and Vietnam: The Roots of Conflict.* Indochina research monograph 1. Berkeley, Calif.: Institute of East Asian Studies, University of California, 1986.

———. *Ho Chi Minh.* New York: Hyperion, 2000.

———. *Vietnam: Nation in Revolution.* Boulder, Colo.: Westview Press, 1983.

Elliot, David W., ed. *The Third Indochina Conflict.* Boulder, Colo.: Westview Press, 1981.

Fall, Bernard. *The Two Vietnams: A Political and Military Analysis.* New York: Praeger Pubs., 1963.

Federal Research Division, Library of Congress. *Vietnam: A Country Study.* Washington, D.C.: U.S. Government Printing Office, 1987.

Garver, John. *Foreign Relations of the People's Republic of China.* Englewood, N.J.: Prentice Hall, 1993.

Gilks, Anne. *The Breakdown of the Sino-Vietnamese Alliance, 1970–1979.* Berkeley, Calif.: Institute of East Asian Studies, University of California, 1992.

Halberstam, David. *Ho.* New York: Vintage Books, 1971.

Hall, D. G. E. *A History of Southeast Asia.* 4th ed. New York: St. Martin's Press, 1981.

Halle, Louis J. *The Cold War as History.* New York: Harper Perennial, 1991.

Hammer, Ellen. *The Struggle for Indochina.* Stanford, Calif.: Stanford University Press, 1954.

Hinton, Harold C. *China's Relations with Burma and Vietnam: A Brief Survey.* New York: Institute of Pacific Research, 1958.

Hood, Steven J. *Dragons Entangled: Indochina and the China-Vietnam War.* New York: M. E. Sharpe, 1992.

Hunt, Michael H. *The Genesis of Chinese Communist Foreign Policy.* New York: Columbia University Press, 1996.

Institute of Southeast Asian Studies. *Southeast Asia Regional Outlook, 2000–2001.* Singapore: ISAS, 2001.

International Monetary Fund. *World Economic Outlook and Statistical Appendix.* Washington, D.C.: IMF, 1999 and 2000 Annual Reports.

Johnson, Lyndon B. *The Vantage Point: Perspectives of the Presidency, 1963–1969.* New York: Holt, Rinehart, and Winston, 1971.

Kenny, Henry J. "The Changing Importance of Vietnam in United States Policy: 1949–1969." Ph.D. Dissertation, American University, 1974.

———. *Possible Threats to Shipping in Key Southeast Asian Sea Lanes.* Alexandria, Va.: Center for Naval Analyses, 1996.

Lawson, Eugene K. *The Sino-Vietnamese Conflict.* New York: Praeger Pubs., 1984.

Library of Congress, Federal Research Division. *Vietnam: A Country Study.* Washington, D.C.: U.S. Government Printing Office, 1989.

Miller, Robert H. *The United States and Vietnam: 1787–1989.* Washington, D.C.: National Defense University Press, 1989.

Noer, John H. *Maritime Interests in the Sea Lines of Communication through the South China Sea.* Washington, D.C.: National Defense University Press, 1997.

Pike, Douglas. *Vietnam and China.* Lubbock, Tex.: The Vietnam Center, Texas Tech University, 1998.

Ross, Robert. *The Indochina Tangle: China's Vietnam Policy, 1975–1979.* New York: East Asia Institute, Columbia University, 1988.

Samuels, Marwyn. *Contest for the South China Sea.* New York: Methuen, 1982.

Smyser, William. *The Independent Vietnamese: Vietnamese Communism between Russia and China 1956–1969.* Athens, Ohio: Center for International Studies, Ohio University.

Stilwell, Joseph. *The Stilwell Papers.* 1948. Reprint, New York: Da Capo Press, 1991.

Taylor, Keith W. *The Birth of Vietnam.* Berkeley, Calif.: University of California Press, 1983.

Thayer, Carlyle A., and Ramses Amer, eds. *Vietnamese Foreign Policy in Transition.* New York: St. Martin's Press, 1999.

Tuchman, Barbara. *Stilwell and the American Experience in China, 1911–1945.* New York: Macmillan Co., 1970.

Tucker, Spencer C. *Vietnam.* Lexington, Ken.: The University of Kentucky Press, 1999.

Vinh, Pham Van. *Vietnam: A Comprehensive History.* Solana Beach, Calif.: PM Enterprises, 1992.

Woodside, Alexander B. *Vietnam and the Chinese Model: A Comparative Study of Vietnamese and Chinese Government in the First Half of the Nineteenth Century.* Cambridge, Mass.: Harvard University Press, 1988.

World Bank. *China 2020: Development Challenges in the New Century.* Washington, D.C.: The World Bank, 1997.

Zhai, Qiang. *China and the Vietnam Wars, 1950–1975.* Chapel Hill, N.C.: University of North Carolina Press, 2000.

Articles

Chinese Ministry of Foreign Affairs. "Declaration of the Government of the People's Republic of China on the Baseline of the Territorial Sea of the People's Republic of China." Beijing: 15 May 1996.

Department of Commerce, Bureau of the Census. "U.S. Trade Balance with China." In *International Trade Statistics.* Washington, D.C.: U.S. Department of Commerce, 2000 and 2001 editions.

Department of Energy, Energy Information Administration. "South China Sea Region." Washington, D.C.: U.S. Government Printing Office, January 2000.

Department of State. "Vietnam: Human Rights Reports for 1999." In *Country Reports on Human Rights Practices.* Washington, D.C.: Department of State, 2000.

Druzek Daniel J. "*Resource Disputes in the South China Sea.*" Conference Report on the South China Sea Conference, Washington, D.C., American Enterprise Institute, 7 September 1994.

Duiker, William, J. "China and Vietnam and the Struggle for Indochina." In *Postwar Indochina: Old Enemies and New Allies,* edited by Joseph J. Zasloff, 147–91. Washington, D.C.: Center for the Study of Foreign Affairs, Foreign Service Institute, Department of State, 1988.

Economic Intelligence Unit (EIU). *China Country Report.* London: EIU, 1999 and 2000, Quarterly Reports.

———. *Vietnam Country Report.* London: EIU, 1999 and 2000, Quarterly Reports.

Hung, Nguyen Manh. "Vietnam in 1999: The Party's Choice." *Asian Survey* (January 2000).

International Monetary Fund. "Vietnam Statistical Appendix and Background Notes." *Staff Report 00/116,* August 2000, 3.

Kenny, Henry J. "The South China Sea: A Dangerous Ground." *Naval War College Review* (Summer 1996).

———. "Vietnamese Perceptions of the 1979 War with China." In *Chinese Warfighting,* edited by Mike McDevitt and Mark Ryan. Armonk, N.Y.: M. E. Sharpe, 2002.

Manyin, Mark E. "The Vietnam-U.S. Bilateral Trade Agreement." Congressional Research Service, 21 July 2000.

Thao, Nguyen Hong. "China's New Advance into the Eastern Sea in 1998." Hanoi *Tap Chi Quoc Phong Toan Dan* (December 1998): 66–68.

Paik, Keun-Wook, and Duk-Ki Kim. "The Spratly Dispute and China's Naval Advance." *Geopolitics of Energy* (1 October 1995).

Pike, Douglas, ed. "Indochina Chronology," Quarterly Reports, 1998–2001. Lubbock, Tex.: The Vietnam Center, Texas Tech University.

———. "Vietnam's Relationship with China." In *Pacific-Asian Issues: American and Chinese Views,* edited by Robert A. Scalipino. Berkeley, Calif.: Institute of East Asian Studies, University of California, 1986.

Shen, Jianming. "International Law Rules and Historical Evidences Supporting China's Title to the South China Sea Islands." Research Paper connected with the Third Annual Conference of Asian Pacific American Law Professors, Los Angeles: University of California, 1996–97.

Thayer, Carlyle. "Regional Rivalries and Bilateral Irritants." *Comparative Connections* (1st Quarter 2001).

United Nations Development Program. *Vietnam Socio-Economic Statistical Bulletin.* February 2000, Part 1.

Womack, Brantly. "Sino-Vietnamese Border Trade: The Edge of Normalization." *Asian Survey* 34, no. 6 (1994): 495–512.

Woodside, Alexander. "Nationalism and Poverty in the Breakdown of Sino-Vietnamese Relations." *Pacific Affairs* 52, no. 3 (1979): 381–409.

World Bank. "Vietnam Attacking Poverty." In *Trends in Poverty, Part 1.* Poverty Working Group, 1999.

INDEX

Page references in **bold** refer to information contained in tables and figures.

171

About the Author

D r. Henry J. Kenny directs studies for the U.S. military at the CNA Corporation in Alexandria, Virginia. He has served with the U.S. Arms Control and Disarmament Agency, the American embassy in Tokyo, and the Senate Foreign Relations Committee. He has also taught undergraduate courses on international relations and problems of developing nations at West Point as well as graduate courses on causes of war and theories of conflict resolution at American and George Washington Universities. A Vietnam veteran, Kenny is the author of *The American Role in Vietnam and East Asia* and other publications. He lives in McLean, Virginia.